Beyond the Pale and Pall of Earthly Reason

Making the Attempt to Ask God

Sean Edward Stewart

Papa Carlo Publishing

Table of Contents

a voice that calls us home

beyond the pale and pall of earthly reason
there is a wind that stirs an honest mind
and on the wind a voice that calls us home
the whispered roar of rolling waters as they leap
and tumble toward innumerable shores
a chant that shatters worlds or makes them whole
like ancient thunder from the nebulae
a Hymn bequeathing all that is or ever
shall be strewn across the lambent sky
to us who once were fashioned from the light
and fired in virtue's womb but now look up
to find ourselves suspended here bereft
between the heat of heaven's engines and
the outer reach of night where nothing burns
to taste antithesis to sound out ignorance
to founder in this elemental sea
until we grasp the outstretched hand of God
and rise to unseen worlds we well remember
there kiss the lips and gaze into the eyes
and sobbing childlike fall upon the necks
of those we loved because they loved us first
who cast us on the waters at our birth

the author

Dedication

This book is dedicated to Governor Menelaus "Pass the Biscuits, Pappy" O'Daniel from the film *O Brother, Where Art Thou?* It was he, who--upon entering a radio station to get out his message, when his feckless son asked if he wasn't going to stop and "press the flesh" with a few bystanders--said, "We ain't one-at-a-timin' here, we're mass communicating."[1]

Preface

This is a collection of true stories: some are inspirational, some are humorous, some are cautionary, but they all revolve around the pivotal moment of my life, when I made the attempt, and asked God in prayer if I should be baptized a member of the Church of Jesus Christ of Latter-day Saints.

As a sometime playwright, the notion of working a few of the events related in this book into a play or perhaps a novel crossed my mind; but haven't we all entertained enough fiction to last us an eternity? Surely there has never been a time in the history of the world when the denizens of this planet were so utterly addicted to fiction: soap operas, sitcoms, TV dramas, films, novels, the "impartial journalism" of the nightly news, comic books and their younger cousin the action movie, Facebook posts, profiles on dating sites, Common Core history lessons, and the crown prince of all fictional genres--reality TV, to name a few. No, I determined to just take a plainspoken account of what occurred and write it down. The events depicted in this book happened exactly as they are related here. No liberties have been taken, artistic or otherwise. I have not embellished anything. As for style, if the reader detects a modicum of flair, I'll be satisfied.

When quotes are employed to denote speech, the maddeningly ubiquitous dialogue tag has been dispatched whenever possible. Where the participants in a conversation are known, and the first to speak has been identified, a close quote followed by an open quote (back to back with no dialogue tag) indicates that the other person is now speaking. When this occurs in series, it means that the two parties to the conversation are alternately speaking. Thus, it should be clear to the reader who is saying what.

Concerning the accuracy of quoted conversations, bear in mind that as a playwright I have an excellent ear and memory for dialogue, not as good as an audio recording, but close. Also, these events have been related countless times over the years with an unshaken consistency; some were recorded in journals, others written down in prepared talks, and a few were so spiritually intense that my memory of them is vivid to this day.

As for a bibliography, I decided to blow it off. If you have any questions concerning the sources behind something I have written, send me an email and I will point you in the right direction. I have included some endnotes, where I considered them to be indispensable; but I wouldn't call that effort rigorous.

And finally, rather than including black and white photos

within, color photos of people and places mentioned in the book may be found on the Facebook page that I have established for readers who wish to follow up with questions and comments (see the afterword for more detail).

About the Author

The author, not having graduated summa cum laude from Harvard University, went on not to pursue postgraduate work at both Oxford and Cambridge. Having been nominated not for a Pulitzer nor a Nobel prize, he understandably won neither; but he considers the non-nomination honor enough. That being said, read the book; you'll learn more than you ever wanted to know about the author. There is but one disclaimer: In writing this book, I neither speak for nor represent the Church of Jesus Christ of Latter-day Saints. I speak only for myself, based on my memory of events and my own understanding.

Acknowledgements

Proceeding on the assumption that the majority of those who assisted me in the preparation of this book for publication would rather not have their names associated with it--and rightly so--I will be thanking them anonymously. As one astute critic pointed out, parts of the book "may generate more heat than light." And even though I took that criticism to heart, dialing back and/or eliminating the more confrontational commentary, in light of the religious nature of the work, I consider such a reaction to be inevitable. Yet, we must not shrink, we who endeavor to speak truth to time-honored albeit erroneous tradition. So, for your invaluable notes, encouragement and editorial prowess, I would like to express my deepest appreciation to all who graciously agreed to read the early drafts. You know who you are.

A Tale of Two Houses

The House of Hipp

After a long pause in a conversation of no real consequence, I peered across the dimly lit cargo van and thought I saw a tear spill down Doug's face. Staring straight ahead, he said, "You know Sean, I'm not happy. There's got to be more to life than this, what we do . . ." We were sitting parked in his driveway that night. I had switched off the engine a while ago. It was quiet. As he spoke, I thought, "You're not happy? Then what chance have the rest of us got?" You see, from my perspective, my friend led an ideal life.

It was the Summer of 1973. Doug had recently graduated from a populous high school where he had been voted senior class president, best-looking and most-likely-to-succeed. He had excelled in sports as the school's star pole-vaulter. He had been accepted to attend the University of Virginia, starting in the fall, where he was destined for Greek life, having served as the president of a local high school fraternity. He could date any girl he wanted. And he was the undisputed leader of our eclectic group of friends who lived in the upper middle-class West End of Richmond, Virginia. Even his last name was cool, Hipp, which coming on the heels of the 60's had considerable cachet.

The Hipps lived in the high-end section of the neighborhood in a large white house, surrounded by old-growth hardwood trees, overlooking a small stream not far

1

from the James River. Doug's father was in the upper tier of management at Reynolds Metals, one of the largest employers in the area. His petite mother was a very social woman, maiden name Cassidy, who had been crowned Miss Aviation USA in her youth, back when Howard Hughes was running TWA. The runner-up in that beauty contest was Dinah Shore. His older brother Donnie was a Ramblin' Wreck from Georgia Tech with a degree in industrial engineering. He dated a smoking hot stewardess named Nan, and drove a green, '68 Corvette that he worked on himself. Then there were his three gorgeous older sisters: Ruthie was everyone's friend and confidant, Barbara was the strikingly sexy one with supermodel good looks, and Donna was a Tri Delta sorority sister and graduate of the University of Alabama. Roll Tide! They were southern royalty; and we, a few of Doug's friends from the neighborhood, took turns playing the role of court jester. The house of Hipp was a happening place, and we hung out there as often as we could.

The House of Stewart

By contrast, my friends rarely even pumped the brakes as they drove past the maelstrom of misery and despair that was my house. My father was a well-educated Southern Baptist minister with a divinity degree from Wake Forest, an engineering degree from NC State (where he studied electrical and nuclear engineering) and a master's from UCLA in cinematography. He was also, without question, the most desperately unhappy man I ever encountered in my life. He made films for the Southern Baptist Convention. After raising her children, my mother got her master's in earth science at Virginia State and taught in public middle school. However wonderfully their marriage may have begun, it devolved until they were locked into some sort of an emotional cage match. There was no winner in the end. They had three children. My older brother, AJ, was a troubled genius with an overactive conscience who was hypersensitive to hypocrisy. He kept to himself a lot. My sister was six years younger than I and going through the awkward braces phase. And that brings us to me, the walking embodiment of great, albeit unrealized potential. AJ and I tried to spend as little time as possible around the house, which left our younger sister there to take the brunt of it. The following is intended to establish the degree to which a sense of hopelessness permeated the home.

It must have been Thanksgiving, or some other holiday, because we were all seated around the large oval table in the formal dining room. My grandfather had come to visit. I was maybe eight years old. My parents, my brother, who was two years older than I, and my sister, who was a toddler at the time, rounded out the room. The adults were having a conversation among themselves, when suddenly my dad's father said, "I'll bet you boys didn't know your father was a murderer." I looked at my father, who had a very violent temper, and saw rage come over his face. My grandfather continued. It seems that when my father was a very young boy, he had been riding his bicycle on the sidewalk. He accidentally ran into a pregnant woman, who subsequently lost the child. My father pulled his right arm back across his chest, showing the back of his hand to my grandfather. He

3

just held it there, for what seemed like a full minute, as my grandfather spoke. My father played a lot of handball. He had powerful arms. Even at my age, I knew that if he unleashed that blow it could easily kill his frail Father, who was in his 70's. Without even looking up from his meal, my grandfather concluded his story, laughed and said, "He won't hit his own father." My dad released the blow, but pulled it short, using the momentum of it to stand suddenly and leave the room, as my grandfather chuckled quietly.

Years later another piece of the puzzle was provided by my grandmother, who had divorced my grandfather years before. About that same time, my father had won a contest in the neighborhood for decorating his bicycle. This was during the Depression. He was so proud, she said. He even got his picture in the paper. She showed me the newspaper clipping. First prize was a wooden model car, a Ford Model A or Model T. By way of punishment for the sidewalk incident, or something else, my grandfather had smashed the model car on the floor and stomped it into kindling wood. Yeah, he was a real piece of work. And my father was an only child. The origins of the frequent fits of anger that he was given to started to come into focus.

To illustrate the nature of my relationship with my father: One day at a high school track meet, after the field events were finished, including my event, my father suddenly appeared. He had come to watch me compete. As he approached, I was observing the last few relay events from the pole-vaulting pit which was located inside the oval. I was surprised to see him there. In the distance a starter pistol sounded, and the crowd let out a roar. When he realized that my event had already finished, he was visibly embarrassed that his effort to support his son had backfired. With an air of resignation, he turned to go and stepped onto the track just as the lead-off runners in the 440 relay came around the turn. I shouted to warn him; but it was too late. One of the young men cursed. My dad, realizing what had happened, froze on the track. To avoid a collision, two of the runners had to break out of their lanes. The sound of disbelief rose up from the crowd in the bleachers. Once they had passed, my dad looked back at me over his shoulder. I'll never forget how utterly crestfallen he was as he walked away. He was so broken up inside, so beaten down by life. My heart ached for him.

Getting Religion

"And I say unto you, Ask, and it shall be given you; seek, and ye shall find; knock, and it shall be opened unto you. For every one that asketh receiveth; and he that seeketh findeth; and to him that knocketh it shall be opened." (Luke 11:9-10)

The Pursuit of Happiness

So, when Doug, with his seemingly perfect family and myriad accolades, tearfully confessed to me that night in the van that he wasn't happy, it got my attention. Everything I thought would make me happy, Doug had. And Doug was not happy. The conversation that night started me on my own personal search for happiness. How was it to be achieved? Could true happiness be sustained, or was it at best fleeting? Was the pursuit of happiness the best we could hope for, because it was, in reality, unattainable? Doug had convinced me that it was not to be found in good looks nor popularity, not in health and youth, not in possessions nor accomplishments nor status of any kind; in short, it was not to be found in anything that the outward world had to offer. So, I turned my attention inward.

A few months after my conversation with Doug (during my senior year of high school), I was at the public library looking at a poster on the bulletin board. It announced (I mistakenly deduced) that the Maharishi Mahesh Yogi was coming to speak later that week on the benefits of

Transcendental Meditation. This was the guru who had taught the Beatles how to meditate. I determined to attend. Of course, in the Maharishi's stead, the pitch was delivered by one of his local devotees, an attractive blonde woman who, although sincere, seemed unsure of herself somehow. She ran through the basics, gave a nod to the Bhagavad Gita, and convinced me to sign up for a private interview with her superior who was to give me my personalized mantra.

Her superior turned out to be a very peaceful, middle-aged black guy with a perpetual smile on his face. He informed me that I would have to forgo any and all foreign substances for two months before receiving my mantra. This was early November. The holidays were just around the corner. Meeting this prerequisite seemed improbable. So, my guide agreed that we should reconvene in March (allowing for two months of sobriety), at which time he conjured up my personalized mantra, "eemah," for a fee of 35 dollars. These two meaningless syllables, chosen specifically for me from the Bhagavad Gita, I would repeat continuously at a slow cadence while in a trancelike state of relaxation for twenty minutes or so, a few times a day. The idea was to follow the mantra back to the frontier of awareness in the mind, whence it came, and then go deeper into "cosmic consciousness." Uncertain whether the benefits derived were the result of the meditation or the sobriety, I was feeling good about it and began to read the Maharishi's English translation of the Bhagavad Gita.

Then one day, I shared my discovery with a girl I was interested in at school, Anita, who was a born-again Christian. She told me that Transcendental Meditation was evil, and that I should read the Bible. This I was not inclined to do, as my father was versed in the Scriptures and they were seemingly incapable of lifting him out of the hell that was his daily existence. And yet, a good-looking girl was talking to me, and she wanted me to read the Bible. So, I read the Bible for the first time in my life, the New Testament, to be precise. And, even though soon thereafter Transcendental Meditation went by the boards, I did continue reading the Bhagavad Gita, at least until it became apparent to me that the Gita was not on the same level as Scripture. The Bible, on the other hand, was having a profound effect on me. Consequently-- notwithstanding my father's miserable example, the many ineffectual years of sermons and Sunday school lessons attended in my youth, and my having been baptized at a young age by Dr. Adams of the First Baptist Church--I began to think of myself for the first time as a Christian.

A Marvelous Work and a Wonder

"If any of you lack wisdom, let him ask of God, that giveth to all men liberally, and upbraideth not; and it shall be given him." (James 1:5)

But Wait, There's More!

Rather than dissecting a frog or taking a derivative somewhere, I was instead creating my own course in comparative religious literature. Unfortunately, this compelling course of study contributed nothing to my grade point average, which took a turn for the worse. In an attempt to salvage my GPA, I dropped my mechanical drawing class (and with it the notion of someday becoming an architect) to pick up a second "study hall." A study hall offered no course material of its own, but was rather a quiet time designed to give students an opportunity to do their homework without the inconvenience of first going home. This particular class met in the cafeteria where we sat on one side only of the long lunch tables, all facing the same direction. No more than three students sat at any one table, making the distance between us considerable; and we had assigned seats. The teacher on duty explained that there would be no talking during the hour, except for the last ten minutes, during which we would be free to converse, but only with the person seated immediately to either side. To my left, no one was assigned to sit. To my right sat Rick Heflebower, the quietest guy I knew. He was positively shy. We ran track together. Doug, Rick, George and I were the four pole-vaulters on the team. My only interaction with Rick occurred during practice and afterwards in the locker room, where the conversation was, in a word, unenlightened, by any standard.

So, when Rick looked over at me during the last ten minutes of class one day and saw me reading the Bible (so much for improving my grades), I'm sure he didn't know what to make of it. He too had an open book in his hands as he asked, "What are you reading?" "The Bible. What about you?" "The Book of Mormon. Do you know what that is?" I did not. Later it became apparent that I had been assigned to sit next to the only active Mormon boy in my high school; but at the time, I didn't even know what a Mormon was. Suddenly, he's telling me about an angel named Moroni that appeared in upstate New York back in the 1800's with an ancient book of scripture engraved on thin sheets of gold. The angel gives the book to a young man named Joseph Smith who is called to be a prophet; he translates the book by the Spirit of God and publishes it as the Book of Mormon, so called because the record was compiled by an ancient American prophet named Mormon. He also told me that he knew the book was true. Where he found the moxie to speak to me about religion at all, much less proselytize, was baffling. Perhaps the shock of seeing me reading the Bible had encouraged him. At any rate, when he finally wound down and seemed to snap out of whatever delusions of missionary fervor he had succumbed to, he said, "So, what . . . uh . . . what do you think about that?" "I don't know, Heflebower, there're angels flying around all over the place in the Bible." "Do you want to read it?" "Sure, give me that thing, I'll read it."

Rick says he didn't see me in that study hall for the next two weeks. All I recall is skipping school to stay home and read the Book of Mormon from cover to cover. I also began praying to know if the book were true. I remember waking up late one morning thinking, "It's third period, chemistry," and then picking up the Book of Mormon to start reading where I had left off the night before. (It was beginning to look like I wasn't going to be a chemist either.) On one such morning, while reading some passage in the Book of Mormon, I felt a remarkable, if fleeting sensation in my chest as the thought came to my mind that the book was in fact true.

The next time my presence graced the halls of Douglas S. Freeman High School, I saw Rick in the hallway. The bell had just rung. There was a sea of youthful humanity churning around us, complete with tides, currents, and eddies. As we were swept past each other, I said over the din, "Hey Heflebower, thanks for that book, man. That thing is true." He seemed momentarily stunned. Then, as the distance between us increased, he shouted, "But wait, there's more!"

A Missionary Drive-By

Not long afterwards, the Heflebowers had me over to their house for dinner. A pair of young Mormon missionaries had also been invited. That night they taught me three full lessons concerning the restored gospel, whereas normally they would only teach one. Then, at their request, I gave the closing prayer. Now, having subsequently served as a full-time missionary, I know what a sure conversion looks like. We call such investigators "golden." I was golden. But these two missionaries never contacted me again.

A year or so later, I ran into one of them walking across the quad at Ricks College, now BYU Idaho. I said, "Hey Elder, do you remember me?" "No." "The Heflebowers, you taught me three lessons, I gave the closing prayer . . ." "Oh, yeah." "What happened to you guys? Why didn't I ever hear from you again?" "Uh . . . we were out of our area, man. We were just there for Sister Heflebower's pies. We passed you on as a referral to the other Elders. Did they not follow up?" "No, no they never did."

I Go a Surfing

It was at that dinner, or thereabouts, that I was given a copy of the Doctrine and Covenants, a compilation of the revelations received by Joseph Smith and a few of his successors, which I began to read. Doug called me around this time and said he had heard that I was getting into something "really strange." I said, "Yeah, so strange I can't even talk about it." The topic was shelved for a later time.

Shortly thereafter, my senior year of high school ended, Doug came home from UVA for the summer, and I registered for summer school in hopes of eventually graduating. But before the summer session started, I decided to go surfing. When Doug heard of my plans over the phone--he'd only been home for about 24 hours--he said he wanted to go. But it was well known that after such a long absence Doug's mom was going to be very covetous of his time. She didn't want to see his friends hanging around her house for at least a week; she wanted him all to herself. So when Doug said he was going surfing with me, I said, "You can't go anywhere. We both know that your mom is gonna . . ." "Just pull up in the driveway. I'll be ready." Hanging up the phone, I thought, "I'm going to tell Doug what's going on." I gathered up my books, loaded the van, picked up Doug, and we were off.

We didn't get into it on the four-hour drive to Hatteras, North Carolina; but when we parked at the lighthouse around midnight and fired up the Coleman stove, I said, "You remember when I told you I was getting into something so strange I couldn't even talk about it?" "Yeah." "Well, this is it." I talked for two hours. Every thirty minutes or so, I'd throw another book at him: New Testament, Book of Mormon, Doctrine and Covenants, and *The Late Great Planet Earth* by Hal Lindsey, which tied then current events to the Book of Revelation. He listened, he perused the books, he asked some good questions. Then a policeman knocked on the van door and told us we couldn't camp there overnight; so we moved on.

Doug and I spent a lot of time that summer holed up in his room studying the Scriptures and praying. Our friends were incredulous. Doug's family were deeply concerned, almost as much so as the time we both had been busted for driving a stolen motorcycle a few years earlier. Right, I'm going to have to tell that story here.

Busted

Doug and I were 15 and 14 years old, respectively. There was a guy in our junior high school named Chat who was the closest thing to James Dean any of us had ever seen. He was in and out of juvenile hall and rarely showed his face at school; he seemed to exist beyond all rules and parental expectations. Chat was in the habit of stealing things, mostly modes of transportation. I ran into him on a trail in the woods one day as he was passing through in a stolen golf cart with a gorgeous girl by his side. But, according to legend, he didn't shrink from bicycles, motorcycles, riding lawn mowers, cars . . . you name it. (Inexplicably, there were no rumors of his stealing a boat or a plane.) He would ride around in or on whatever he could find until it broke down or ran out of gas; then he would hike out of there and steal something else.

As you might expect, Chat had groupies that worshiped at his feet. There was one group of kids, who were several years younger, that would follow him around and scoop up whatever they found in his wake. We heard that they had taken possession of a 175 CC Honda motorcycle. Knowing where they kept their stash in the woods, we snuck in there and took it from them.

From there we rode the bike all over the West End until we eventually found ourselves at the corner of Parham Road and Patterson Avenue, waiting in a long line of cars at the stoplight. Suddenly, up ahead, we saw a motorcycle cop pull into the middle of the intersection and stop traffic in all four directions. Then he looked directly at us. Virginia had just passed a helmet law, and we were not wearing helmets; but that was the least of our worries. We didn't have a driver's license between us, and the bike was stolen. We weren't even wearing shoes. Knowing that we were busted, we got off the bike and pushed it to the side of the road to wait for the officer. Then, miraculously, he continued straight ahead traveling west on Patterson. He was leading a funeral! We were spared.

We got back on the bike and made a beeline for Doug's house. His older brother Donnie was there. He wanted to know where we got the bike. After hearing our story, he said, "That's great, until you get caught." We scoffed at the notion. But just to be safe, we decided to stay off the roads for a while. We took the bike down to Bosher's dam in the bottomland along the James River. There we raced back and forth on the dirt roads until the bike was almost out of gas. I was driving as we made our way back to Doug's house which was just across the street. As we approached River Road, steering around the brick and metal gates there that never kept us out, I looked left, and then as I looked right, the same motorcycle cop glided to a stop beside us. He uncapped his shades and said, "You boys were at the corner of Parham and Patterson about two hours ago, weren't you?" We were too stunned to react. Twenty minutes later I was sitting in the back of a squad car in the Hipp's driveway while an officer explained our crimes to Mr. and Mrs. Hipp. The garage door opened and Donnie stood there shaking his head with an expression that read, "What did I say?"

We sang like canaries. Both of us gave up Chat in a heartbeat. One more trip to juvenile hall wasn't going to make any difference to him. Since we hadn't actually stolen the bike, we both got the proverbial slap on the wrist. Still, I didn't hang around the Hipp household for a while after that. They considered me a bad influence on their son. But, if it please the court, let the record show, that was a two-way street.

Knock, and It Shall Be Opened

Now, fast forward three years, and even though my "influence" was at the opposite end of the behavioral spectrum, the reaction from Doug's family was more or less the same, "What's he got them into now?" To answer that question, after all our study and prayer, we were leaning heavily towards the Mormons, as their theology incorporated the truths found in all the other churches of Christendom, and adequately explained their existence, while the rest of Christendom rejected the additional truths of the latter-day restoration, and had no plausible explanation for Mormonism.

School was about to start, and we were running out of books to read. Heflebower was still missing in action, having gone off somewhere for most of the summer. Knowing where the Mormon church was down on Monument Avenue, I stopped by on a weekday and knocked on the door. A ward clerk named Rick Gunn opened and asked how he could help. When he heard that I had read the Book of Mormon and the Doctrine and Covenants, and had come to the chapel looking for something else to read, he invited me in. He gave me the first three volumes of a seven-volume set of LDS church history which, among other sources, drew from Joseph Smith's journals. He also wrote down my name, address, and phone number, saying he would have the missionaries contact me. And it was about time.

Making the Attempt

"So, in accordance with this, my determination to ask of God, I retired to the woods to make the attempt . . . It was the first time in my life that I had made such an attempt, for amidst all my anxieties I had never as yet made the attempt to pray vocally." (Joseph Smith History 1:14)

The Missionaries, Take Two

It was September of 1974. Doug had gone back to UVA, where he was living in a frat house. I was postponing college, much to my parents' dismay, in an attempt to adjust to a completely new Weltanschauung. (Sorry, I've just always wanted to use that word in a sentence. Coming from the German, of course, it literally translates to "worldview," but carries the connotation of an all-encompassing conception of the universe and how humanity relates to it.)

Then one day, as I was reading LDS church history, a pair of young Mormon missionaries knocked on my door, Elder Bill Billingsly from Billings, Montana (you can't make this stuff up), and Elder Betticker. They would teach me the basics of Church doctrine, and I would teach them the finer points of Church history. It didn't bother me that they were not gospel scholars; when they came through the door, the Spirit of God came with them. The Elders taught me many important truths. I was a little worried about Elder Betticker though. I had recently read in Isaiah where the prophet had chastised the "daughters of Zion" for their vanity in wearing "earrings, rings and nose jewels."[2] Then Elder Betticker told me he wanted to be a jeweler someday. I thought he was on the highroad to apostasy. (As the remainder of these events unfolds, you will realize that the words that best characterize my early days in the Church are: well-meaning, but overzealous.) Fortunately, this didn't interfere with our course of study, and eventually the Elders challenged me to be baptized. I told them I would pray about it.

A Conversation with God

It seems absurd in retrospect, but at the time, it struck me as odd that these Mormons were all the way out in Virginia. Perhaps they were an apostate splinter group. Maybe I needed to go to Utah to get the straight juice. I mean, there was that whole business with Elder Betticker wanting to be a jeweler. And I had observed Rick's father drink a Coke® with his meal, which I erroneously had been led to believe was verboten. So, that was my mindset as I made the attempt to ask God if I should be baptized and become a Latter-day Saint.

Additionally, I had taken the following scripture to heart, Doctrine and Covenants 9:8-9, "But, behold, I say unto you, that you must study it out in your mind; then you must ask me if it be right, and if it is right I will cause that your bosom shall burn within you; therefore, you shall feel that it is right. But if it be not right you shall have no such feelings, but you shall have a stupor of thought that shall cause you to forget the thing that is wrong."

With that in mind, I made sure I was alone in the house,

went to my room, knelt down, closed my eyes, and bowed my head. Then I spoke the following words aloud, "Dear Father in heaven, should I be baptized into The Church of Jesus Christ of Latter-day Saints in Richmond, Virginia . . ."

At that precise moment, I was overcome by an experience that is nearly impossible to describe. Over the years, I've tried to put it into words, and this is the best I've come up with. It was as though a small portion of the sun had coalesced in my chest, radiating light, love and intelligence through my entire being with a remarkable intensity. The Spirit of Truth that flowed into me came not from without, but from within. Having experienced it, I understand how it came to be known as a burning in the bosom, even though there was no actual heat involved. I remained on my knees with tears flowing down my face. I have no idea how long this lasted. Eventually the experience subsided, and I was left as I had been before. But, wanting to be thorough, I thought I should ask the other half of my question (as if anything might top what had just occurred). And so, I cleared my throat and said, "Or . . . should I go to . . . to . . . uh . . ." I could not remember the name of the state. I knew it had four letters. I knew it was near Wyoming. But for the life of me, I could not conjure the name of a state of the Union. Then, remembering the "stupor of thought" mentioned in the scripture quoted above, I thought, "Well, I hope that's what this is." After abandoning the notion of continuing my prayer, immediately the name of the state, Utah, came to my mind. The Elders were thrilled to hear of my experience. A date was set for my baptism on November 9th, 1974, a Saturday evening.

A Broken Heart and a Contrite Spirit

"Behold, he who has repented of his sins, the same is forgiven, and I, the Lord, remember them no more. By this ye may know if a man repenteth of his sins--behold, he will confess them and forsake them." (Doctrine and Covenants 58:42-43)

Repentance

There followed two baptismal interviews which necessitated my confessing a considerable list of transgressions, of which I had only recently repented. This admission is not to suggest that I was guilty of any heinous crimes. I had not, nor could I ever, intentionally do anything to hurt anyone in any way; but my confession covered things that were at odds with the better angel of my nature. The first interview was with one of the young Elders who held a leadership position in the mission field, and it was somewhat perfunctory. But he said something that came as a revelation to me, and I responded, "You mean, I can be a missionary? I can go out and do what you're doing?" He looked surprised and said, "Yes." I couldn't think of anything I would rather do. But first, there was the matter of my baptism. The second interview was with the Bishop of the ward, and although it was a little more in depth, he wasn't overly interested in the details. Still, it was difficult to confess to this good brother every activity from my past that was contrary to the high gospel standards I was about to embrace; but I didn't keep anything hidden from him.

To put it bluntly, no one who knew me in my youth thought for a moment that I was in any danger of getting religion. It certainly came as a shock to me. Likewise, those who came to know me only after my baptism, due to the thoroughness of the transformation I had undergone, had difficulty believing just how misspent my youth had been. Once a friend, a convert who was privy to my former waywardness, told me this story. He was sitting in a testimony meeting where I was speaking of my conversion when a girl leaned over to him and said, "Wow, Sean must have been a real straight arrow before he joined the Church." My friend, somehow managing not to laugh out loud, said, "No, not really." Furthermore, those who read this book and conclude that after my conversion I had overcome the world and never again strayed from the path would also be wrong. So, despite the fact that some of these stories make me look like a prince, trust me, there are others I could share that would leave you with a very different impression. By way of example, the following is included to render the subsequent and more spiritual events of my teenage years in high relief.

But for the Grace of God

I was driving home one night after a date. There was a light rain falling. The car windows were fogged up on the inside. A half-empty bottle of Boone's Farm wine was rolling around on the floorboard. This was Richmond, Virginia, 1972. I was sixteen years old and driving my grandmother's brand-new Pontiac Grand Prix for the first time. The road I was on has since been straightened out, but back then it was a real roller-coaster ride that cut through the heart of an enclave in the West End where all the black families lived. We called it Ziontown. It was wooded and wild and most of the houses sat on a full acre of land or more. I knew the area well. It was just through the woods from Roslyn Hills, the well-manicured, all-white neighborhood where I lived. I had wandered around Ziontown at all hours of the day and night for years, either on foot, a bicycle, or a minibike.

So, it wasn't that the road was unfamiliar to me that night, and I hadn't had much to drink; but then I wasn't a very accomplished drinker. It was dark, but not terribly late. For whatever reason, I either just left the road, passed out or fell asleep at the wheel. When I woke up, the car was in a ditch. I had hit my head on the dome light and smashed it. The bottle of Boone's Farm had shattered. Broken glass and wine were everywhere. My head was throbbing with pain. I got out and checked the car. The front left tire was completely flat, it looked like the frame was bent, and the engine wouldn't start. It was bad. I had come to rest in someone's front yard. The house was well back from the street, but I could hear music playing up there.

As I drew closer and looked around the corner of the house, I saw four or five middle-aged black couples having a dance party on a covered patio in the backyard that was fenced in. Realizing that flinging open the gate and saying "Hello" probably wouldn't go over that well, I went to the front porch and rang the bell. An elderly black man opened the door. I told him that I had crashed my car on his front lawn. He came a little closer, looked over my shoulder at the wrecked car, sniffed the air, and asked, "You been drinking?" "Yes, sir." "All right, come on in." He produced two cigarettes, snapped the filters off and held them up to my face, saying, "Here, chew on this. The tobacco takes the smell of alcohol off your breath." I knew immediately I was in good hands and began to chew. I told him about the broken wine bottle. He put some water in a bucket, and then grabbed a sponge and a flashlight.

It was still drizzling rain when we got to the car and he shone his light on the flat front tire. I could see a flap of rubber where there was a large slice in the tread. With his flashlight, he followed the tire track in the mud back about 40 feet to a corrugated steel pipe that ran under his neighbor's driveway. It was obvious that the edge of the pipe had cut my tire as I left the road. He said, "OK, here's what you say. You were driving down the road in the rain, when you heard a loud pop, and the car pulled hard to the left. Next thing you know, you're in the ditch. You had a blowout, son. That's what it was, a blowout." "Yeah, OK, that's sounds good." We cleaned up the broken glass, and wiped the splattered wine off the interior. Then it was up to the house to make phone calls.

My parents got there before the police. I was cold sober as I told them my story. Then the officer took his flashlight out, and I thought I was done. Fortunately, though, he didn't have as much sense as my elderly black friend. Instead of following the tire track back to where I left the road, he shined the light on the sliced tire and said, "Oh yeah, looks like dry rot. I've seen this before." Someone commented that it was a good thing it happened to me that night, and not to grandma the next day as she drove home to North Carolina. Suddenly I was a hero. About a year or so later, grandma came for a visit and said to me, "Strangest thing, I got a letter from my insurance company saying they had proven in court that that tire didn't have dry rot. It was cut, they said." "Huh, that's odd." I think I was in my late twenties before I told anyone in my family what happened that night.

It's obvious to me that God was watching over me long before I sought him out. I easily could have crossed the line that night and killed a young mother with her four children in a head-on collision. I could have cut down a pedestrian walking by the side of the road. I could have hit a tree and been paralyzed, or killed, or left in a mentally diminished state. I'm sure there are people who have served time in prison for doing nothing more than I did that night. "There, but for the grace of God, go I."

Baptism and
the Gift of the Holy Ghost

"And they said one to another, Did not our heart burn within us, while he talked with us by the way, and while he opened to us the scriptures?" (Luke 24:32)

The Waters of Baptism

My family had shown no interest in the restored gospel, despite my repeated attempts to share it with them. As a result, assuming they would not be interested, I failed to invite them to my baptism, which I very much regret. I had observed someone else join the Church during my studies with the missionaries, as I was attending Sunday services during that time. This individual was baptized on a Saturday evening, and then confirmed, i.e., given the gift of the Holy Ghost by the laying on of hands, the following day in front of the congregation. The natural assumption was that my baptism would follow that paradigm. So, at the appointed time, I gathered my white clothing, in which I was to be baptized, and--thinking no one would see me in any other clothing--put on a pair of oil-stained blue jeans, an old sweatshirt, and motorcycle boots, for the ride to the chapel on my BSA 450 "Shooting Star" motorcycle.

That night there was another young man, about my age, there to be baptized. As we got to know each other in our white clothes prior to the service, I thought, "This guy and

I will probably be friends for life." He wasn't at church for the next few Sundays. Then we bumped into one another at Regency Square Mall. I asked him how he'd been, and why he wasn't coming to church. He said, "Oh no, that's not for me. I found a faith healer out in Goochland, man. He's the real deal. He's got the Spirit." "Oh. So, I won't be seeing you around then." I never saw him again.

When it was my turn, having stepped down into the baptismal font, the Elder standing beside me raised his hand to the square and said, "Having been commissioned of Jesus Christ, I baptize you in the name of the Father, and of the Son, and of the Holy Ghost. Amen." In light of my previous experience, while praying to know if I should be baptized, the expectation that something truly remarkable would happen at my baptism was inevitable. So, understandably, coming up out of the water feeling . . . wet, but not much more, was a little disappointing. Still, there was no question in my mind that I had done the right thing. Then, while drying off and getting dressed for the ride home, someone mentioned that everyone was waiting for me in the junior Sunday school room, where I was to be confirmed. I said, "No, that's tomorrow, isn't it?" "No, that's tonight." So, I put on my dry clothes, such as they were, and walked down the hall to the other room.

The Laying On of Hands

Entering the back of the junior Sunday school room, the scene before me was somewhat surreal in that the occupied chairs were of normal size, but the empty ones were those little children's chairs. It gave the illusion that everyone was sitting on one of those tiny little chairs. I was surprised at how many people were in attendance, especially when they all turned around to look at me as I tromped up to the front in my jeans, sweatshirt, and motorcycle boots. What they must have been thinking?

I was 6'1" and athletic; but the men who stood in a circle around the chair at the front of the room were barrel-chested Virginia farmers and workers with big gnarly hands and broad shoulders. Men with names like Henshaw and Powers. I never felt more like a boy among men in my life. I sat in the chair, and these brothers who held the priesthood closed the circle around me. There were so many of them that each one could only put his right hand on my head, the other hand was placed on the right shoulder of the brother standing to the left.

At this point my heart was racing uncontrollably. It was pounding in my ears so rapidly and with such force that I literally could not hear. Brother Goodson, a member of the ward bishopric, began to confirm me a member of the Church. He was standing directly behind me. His mouth was no more than three feet from my ears, and undoubtedly, he was speaking up so everyone in the room could hear. But I couldn't make out a single syllable. Through the relentless thumping in my ears, I heard only a muffled murmuring sound. Being concerned that I might not hear anything he would say, I prayed silently, "Lord, this is a blessing of some kind. Shouldn't I be able to hear this?" At that exact moment, my heart--which must have been beating 150 times a minute--abruptly slowed to my normal resting heart rate. This happened in the interval between one beat and the next. I was suddenly bathed in serenity; and I heard with crystal clarity the words, ". . . receive the Holy Ghost." The burning in my bosom returned, though it was noticeably less intense than it had been previously. The other difference being that on this occasion it did not subside as it had before, but instead remained with me, and I gradually became accustomed to it.

I heard every word of the blessing after that. And I now know, having subsequently confirmed others myself, that the words brother Goodson spoke which I could not hear, were more or less these, "Brother Sean Edward Stewart, by virtue of the Melchisedek priesthood which we hold, we, the Elders of Israel, lay our hands upon your head, and confirm you a member of The Church of Jesus Christ of Latter-day Saints, and we say unto you (then the first words I heard) receive the Holy Ghost."

A Letter to Doug

As I returned home on the night of my baptism, my parents and my sister were having a late dinner in the kitchen. I walked past the open doorway and started up the stairs carrying a bundle of wet white clothing. The question came, "Where have you been?" "I was baptized tonight." Silence. Once in my room, I sat down to write a letter to Doug, which began, "If I have ever written anything under the influence of the Holy Ghost, this is it."

I had found the wellspring of all happiness in the restored gospel of Jesus Christ. Having heard the word of God preached: I had believed in the atonement, humbled myself through the process of repentance, and done the will of the Father--following the example of His only begotten Son--to be baptized by one holding the holy priesthood. And, most importantly, I had received the gift of the Holy Ghost by the laying on of hands from God's authorized servants. And thus, by embracing the restored gospel and joining with His saints in the latter days, I had entered in at the strait gate, which is the most crucial part of God's plan of happiness for his children. Now, all that was left for me to do was "endure to the end" and "press forward with a steadfastness in Christ, having a perfect brightness of hope, and a love of God and of all men." (2 Nephi 31:20)

A Flash Forward

Doug soon began meeting with the missionaries in Charlottesville. He was baptized about six months after I was, and subsequently served a full-time mission as a Spanish-speaking Elder in the Tempe, Arizona Mission. Doug, Rick and I were all in the mission field at the same time. We swapped letters encouraging one another in the work. Rick got home first, from the Independence, Missouri Mission, and didn't waste any time convincing a young beauty named Sue to marry him in the Washington, DC temple--not so shy anymore. They raised four children in the Church and now live near St. George, Utah. Rick has served for a total of ten years between the Bishopric and the High Council. After his mission, Doug returned to Richmond where he shared the restored gospel with Pam Nalle, his girlfriend from junior high school. (I remember when they first "went steady.") After she investigated the Church for a few months, Doug baptized her, and I confirmed her a member of the Church. They got married soon after that, and were then sealed in the Washington, DC temple for time and eternity. Doug's mother also joined the Church after a few years. Today Doug and Pam live near Memphis, where they raised four children in the Church. Doug was recently released after serving for seventeen years between the Bishopric and the High Council.

An Observation

While my experiences with the Holy Ghost may seem remarkable to some, even to some members of the Church, they are by no means unique. Such experiences, and others that utterly eclipse anything that has ever happened to me, are commonplace in the Church. I am aware of Latter-day Saints who have seen visions in the open air, dreamed prophetic dreams, heard an audible voice giving instructions in answer to prayer, healed the sick, prophesied, spoken in tongues, communed with spiritual beings from the other side of the veil, and so on. All the gifts of the Spirit that were manifest in the Biblical Church of Christ are found in His restored Church in our day. "God is the same yesterday, today and forever."

And yet, there are those in the Church who have longed

for such overt spiritual experiences and not had them. This gives rise to the question, why me? It is tempting to believe that it is the natural consequence of personal merit. Knowing myself as I do, this is laughable. Sometimes (and I'm not being facetious), I think a few of the more interesting events of my life occurred because God knew in His foresight that I was going to write a book someday, and He wanted me to have something to work with. As for the more spiritual events, I believe that members of the Church who have such overt experiences in our day, have them either because God knows that they will need them to endure to the end, as they often are coming from a dark place and have no spiritual support system in their lives, or, they are just experiencing the same thing differently because they have never encountered anything like it before. Conversely, those who have been raised in the Church have generally grown up in a supportive family and lived under the influence of the Holy Ghost from their mother's womb. As a result, when they receive the gift of the Holy Ghost it has a far less palpable impact on them. And when they seek confirmation of their beliefs, though the Spirit of Truth flows into them from within in the same manner, they more often merely perceive the still small voice of the Spirit, with which they are already familiar, subtly speaking peace to their minds. Imagine being in a brightly lit room where the rheostat is set at 8 out of 10. Increasing the intensity of the light by rolling it up to 10 is barely perceptible. Now imagine being in a room that is nearly dark when you crank it up to 10 in an instant. It is blinding, and results in a far more visceral reaction.

Additionally, there seems to be a principle at work here that the Lord enunciated in John 20:29, "Jesus saith unto him, Thomas, because thou hast seen me, thou hast believed: blessed are they that have not seen, and yet have believed." In other words, the magnitude of the blessings that come as a result of one's faith in Christ, is inversely proportional to how conspicuous a manifestation is required to engender that faith in that individual in the first place. Simply put, more overt manifestations may not be in one's best interest. Apparently, this principle holds true until one's faith approaches certain knowledge, and then it's moot.

Those of us who have a more jarring introduction to God's Spirit, with the passage of time, reach a certain spiritual equilibrium. From the days of my conversion to the writing of this book, having become accustomed to the continuing presence of the Spirit in my life, whenever I have experienced a burning in my bosom the intensity of the sensation has been far, far subtler than that which I experienced when it was all new to me. In fact, over the years that I have been a member of the Church, the only spiritual earthquakes that have rivaled what happened to me in the beginning occurred when I was unworthy, and the Holy Ghost withdrew from me. That's a bad, bad feeling. But Christ's atonement enables us to repent. That's why we meet on Sunday to partake of the Sacrament. It allows us to renew the covenants that we made in the waters of baptism, and be cleansed anew, so that the Holy Ghost can return and dwell within us, and we can try again to keep God's commandments.

For those who aren't steeped in religiosity, allow me to put it in other words which are devoid of religious jargon. Think of the gift of the Holy Ghost as receiving a perfect spiritual being into your innermost self, one who: cleanses your "heart" by wiping out years of dark thoughts and deeds from your subconscious; sheds light on every aspect of your life; fills you with faith, hope, and love; becomes your personal life coach, counselor and comforter going forward; and jacks you into the mainframe computer in the sky. Over time, you become a new person; one who is more intelligent, more faithful, more hopeful, more empathetic, wiser, healthier, with patience and long-suffering toward all. One former prophet and president of the Church, David O. MacKay, even suggested that the Holy Ghost's daily influence on our thoughts actually refines one's appearance.[3] But then how could it not, having taken upon oneself the countenance of the Savior?

I feel compelled to add that having had experiences with the Holy Ghost, and then subsequently having received the gift of the Holy Ghost, I understand the significant difference between the two. The late Elder Bruce R. McConkie, of the Quorum of the Twelve Apostles, explained the difference as well as anyone can. He compared a manifestation of the Holy Ghost--that one may receive before baptism and the laying on of hands--to "a flash of lightning blazing forth in a dark and stormy night." He compared the gift of the Holy Ghost--that one may only receive by the laying on of hands after baptism--to "the continuing blaze of the sun at noonday, shedding its rays on the path of life and on all that surrounds it."[4]

The Recent Convert

"Behold, I sent you out to testify and warn the people, and it becometh every man who hath been warned to warn his neighbor." (Doctrine and Covenants 88:81)

Patience and Long-Suffering

I walked into the chapel on Monument Avenue one Sunday and spotted brother Ted Lansing seated on the back row by the door, writing something on a notepad. He had recently been released from the Stake Presidency and subsequently called to be the ward scoutmaster. I didn't fully comprehend that this was the real-world equivalent of being demoted from CEO to working in the mailroom. (Not that we think of it in those terms; in all humility, I'm sure he was just as happy to be working with the Scouts as he had been to sit in the high councils of the local Church, perhaps more so.) Wanting to congratulate him on his new calling, but being unfamiliar with LDS nomenclature, I walked up to where he was seated and said, "So, I hear you've been set aside." He looked up at me as though he were thinking, "Is he yanking my chain, or does he just not know?" He apparently concluded that it was the latter and said, "That's . . . uh . . . 'set apart,' Sean. I've been set apart." "Oh, right. So, what are you working on?" "I'm just making some notes. I'm going to be speaking here in a few minutes." I was appalled. I reminded him of the scripture found in Doctrine and Covenants 84:85 which reads, "Neither take ye thought beforehand what ye shall say; but treasure up in your minds continually the words of life, and it shall be given you in the very hour that portion that shall be meted unto every man." Again, he looked up at me with those eyes full of patience and long-suffering, and again he came down on the side of charity, saying, "Well, Sean, the Scriptures also say, 'Prepare every needful thing' . . . and I need these notes, so . . ." And I thought, "Huh, touché."

Soon after that, a member of the Bishopric asked me to give my first talk in church. It was supposed to be 15 to 20 minutes in length. I remember thinking, "I'll show them how it's done." Accordingly, I made no preparation whatsoever, but instead put my trust in the Spirit to give me in the moment the words that God would have me speak. Once at the podium, I announced as much to the congregation. This was followed by three, no more than four minutes of aimless rambling, after which I made another announcement, that the Spirit was not giving me anything. Then I sat down. Bishop Barry Mills called me into his office after the meeting and said, "I don't understand, Sean. You were doing so well. What happened?" A year and a half passed before they asked me to speak again; and then they had to let me talk because it was my missionary farewell.

This May Sound Strange to You

Several months after my baptism, I was feeling discouraged that so few people were taking an interest in the pearl of great price that I had discovered. I actually went around to my neighbors and told them they needed to repent and join the LDS church. They listened politely and showed me the door. This was before Doug was baptized; he was still up at UVA. Most of my friends in town had written me off as "strange" or "no fun anymore." So, one Friday night, my prayers included a simple request, that God would send me a friend, someone who would be receptive to the restored gospel. It was one line in a five-minute prayer before I crawled into bed and thought no more about it.

The next morning, I woke up to an empty house. Whatever my plans were that Saturday, when I went to start my motorcycle, it became apparent that the battery had corroded overnight, which struck me as odd. I took the battery out, put it in a paper bag, and started walking and/or hitchhiking to Cliff's motorcycle shop on Cary Street to buy a new one. I walked through the neighborhoods all the way to River Road before getting my first ride. Nothing about the driver was memorable, except that he dropped me off not far from the foot of the Huguenot Bridge, in front of the Exxon station that used to be there.

After standing by the side of the road for a few minutes with my thumb out, in the distance, a green Land Rover jeep came down the ramp from the bridge. I thought, "This guy is going to stop for me. He drives a jeep with a winch on the front; there's probably extra gas in a can strapped to the back--he likes to help people." Sure enough, the jeep rolled to a stop beside me. I got in and thanked the driver for the ride. He was about my age and looked like he could have been one of the Beach Boys. He said his name was Mike. I said, "Sean."

We shook hands, I told him my destination, and we started up the hill past the Country Club of Virginia toward Cary Street.

There was a brief silence. The next words out of his mouth were these: "This may sound strange to you, but as I was coming off of the bridge, I saw you thumbing, and I thought, I'll pick this guy up and see if he has anything to say about religion." Then he looked at me. My prayer from the night before came to mind. He continued, "You see, I've been praying a lot lately. I had an appointment with my minister today. I waited 45 minutes, but he never showed up; and now I'm on my way home. And I really had my heart set on getting some answers about religion today." Then he looked at me again. At that point, no doubt much to his surprise, I said, "Yes, I do have something to say about religion."

I told him that back in the 1800's there was a young man named Joseph Smith in upstate New York who also very much wanted to get some answers about religion. I told him about Joseph's first vision in which he spoke with the Father and the Son. I told him about the angel Moroni and the Book of Mormon. At one point, he put his hand over his heart and interrupted me, saying, "Wait a minute. I don't know why, but as I've listened to you talk, I've felt the most wonderful feeling here in my chest." I was feeling it too. I told him that what he was experiencing was the Holy Ghost bearing witness of the truth, and that I too had experienced it when these things were made known to me. And with that, we looked up to find we had arrived at Cliff's motorcycle shop. Mike pulled off onto the shoulder. He gave me his contact information, and I promised to get him a copy of the Book of Mormon. To this day, I can see the scene clearly, standing behind the jeep as he checked his side view mirror and pulled back into traffic. Whether or not I bought a new battery, I don't recall. I can't remember how I got home that day. But those ten minutes in that jeep with Mike are indelibly etched on my soul.

We got to know each other over the coming weeks. He was a musician, mostly electric guitar. I dropped by his house and we hung out. Mike started meeting with the missionaries; but after only two lessons he got a gig for the summer in Virginia Beach playing lead guitar in a Beach Boys knockoff band. By the time he got back, I was in Rexburg, Idaho attending Ricks College for one semester before going off to serve a full-time mission. We lost touch with one another. It was easier to do in the 70's; there was no Facebook and there were no smartphones. As a result, to this day I have no idea what became of him. What he did with that experience we shared--whether or not he was baptized into the Church--I don't know. I have tried several times over the years to track him down, with no success. So, Mike, if you are out there somewhere reading this, send up a flare. I would love to catch up.

An Observation

Afterwards, I thought, what a fine prayer I offered that night. But with time, I realized that it had been Mike's prayers that brought us together that day. I suspect that I was tapped to play a role in answering his prayers because God knew that I would respond with a bold declarative statement of truth, one that the Holy Ghost could bear witness to.

I often marvel at all the work on the other side of the veil that must have gone into getting the two of us in the same place at the same time that day. First, I was prompted to offer my little prayer. Then my battery had to corrode overnight. Next, someone had to take out Mike's minister. Who knows? Was it a flat tire? Maybe he had intended to play only nine holes, but--with a little help from above--he was seven under at the turn and had to finish the round for a personal best; we'll never know. Then that first driver had to stop and give me a ride, dropping me off directly in Mike's path a few minutes before he came over the bridge. Mike had to be prompted to pick me up and tell me what was on his mind. After that, all that was left was for me to open my mouth and share the restored gospel, and for the Holy Ghost to bear witness of the truth.

I wonder if there is anyone reading this who is cynical enough to think that my meeting Mike that day was a mere coincidence, or worse yet, the work of the devil. Really? You think the devil intercepted a Christian's earnest prayers-- which were offered to the Father in the name of the Son, and in keeping with the promise found in James 1:5--and then, God stood idly by as Satan deceived him into believing the "damnable lies" of Joseph Smith by replicating the very burning in the bosom that the two disciples on the road to Emmaus had experienced, which they took as confirmation that they indeed had been speaking with the resurrected Savior? Really? Well, if you're reading this, and that's what you get out of it, my question to you is: Do you actually believe that Satan is more powerful than God? Consider this: "Or what man is there of you, whom if his son ask bread, will he give him a stone? Or if he ask a fish, will he give him a serpent? If ye then, being evil, know how to give good gifts unto your children, how much more shall your Father which is in heaven give good things to them that ask him?" (Matthew 7:9-11)

Ah, Zion!

I took a bus across country to check out Ricks College in Rexburg, Idaho. Even though it sounded more like a bar and grill, my parents were thrilled that I was considering college at all. On the way out there, my trip included a couple of days in Salt Lake City. I stepped out of the bus station into the sunlight in downtown Salt Lake looking like a new penny, took a deep breath of mountain air, and thought, "Ah, Zion!" Just then an old derelict that was sitting on a bench nearby whistled at me; you know, as a sailor whistles at a dame. To say the illusion was shattered would be an understatement. I hurried to the Hotel Utah and got some much needed sleep. The next day, while walking around Temple Square, some locals befriended me, a young Latter-day Saint couple, Dan Grover and his fiancé. When they heard my story, and learned that I was staying in the hotel, they insisted that I spend the next night with them. So, I checked out of the hotel and sister Grover put me up for the night. Their hospitality was overwhelming. Finally arriving in Idaho, Ricks College made such a favorable impression on me that I started the enrollment process immediately.

We Thank Thee, O God, for a Prophet

I had missed out on the dedication of the Washington, DC Temple, which took place ten days after my baptism. Someone asked me if I were going to attend, and I said no, having not heard about it and not understanding what it was. Someone should have grabbed me by the lapels and said, "You need to be there for this!" I was, however, convinced to attend "The Hill Cumorah Pageant" in upstate New York in the summer of 1975. It represents the coming forth of the Book of Mormon, and some of its contents.

I remember one beautiful, clear, somewhat windy day during the event. I was one of a large group of young Latter-day Saints gathered together from all over the US and Canada, some to participate, others to watch. Elder Marion G. Romney, a member of the Quorum of the Twelve Apostles, was there to address us. He was nearly eighty years old at the time, and the wind was whipping his white hair around his head while he told us this story from his life. As a young man, he had visited some famous caverns, either Luray caverns in the Shenandoah or someplace like it. At one point in the tour the guide paused and asked for a volunteer to sing so that the cavern's famous echo might be demonstrated. The Spirit whispered to Marion, "Go up there and sing 'We Thank Thee, O God, for a Prophet.'" Despite having a good singing voice, he thought, "No, I don't want to sing." The Spirit again urged him to step forward and sing. But he didn't. No one came forward, the moment passed, and the tour moved on. And now, some sixty years later, what was on the apostle's mind? Who in the crowd that day was supposed to have heard "We Thank Thee, O God, for a Prophet," but didn't, because he failed to step up? The words of the hymn (which were written by William Fowler, 1830-1865) may be found in any LDS hymnal.

We thank thee, O God, for a Prophet
To guide us in these latter days.
We thank thee for sending the gospel
To lighten our minds with its rays.
We thank thee for every blessing
Bestowed by thy bounteous hand.
We feel it a pleasure to serve thee
And love to obey thy command.

When dark clouds of trouble hang o'er us
And threaten our peace to destroy,
There is hope smiling brightly before us,
And we know that deliverance is nigh.
We doubt not the Lord nor his goodness.
We've proved him in days that are past.
The wicked who fight against Zion
Will surely be smitten at last

We'll sing of his goodness and mercy.
We'll praise him by day and by night,
Rejoice in his glorious gospel,
And bask in its life-giving light.
Thus on to eternal perfection
The honest and faithful will go,
While they who reject this glad message
Shall never such happiness know.

I rarely get through the final verse without choking on tears, thinking about my family and friends who have indeed rejected "this glad message." Often a nightmarish scenario plays out in my mind. I am walking ten or twelve abreast in the midst of an innumerable host of the faithful from all ages of the earth's history. We are approaching one of the twelve gates which lead into the Celestial City as described in the Book of Revelation. Over each gate is carved the name of one of the twelve patriarchs of Israel (all sons of a polygamous marriage, by the way, so yeah, there's that). Lining the road are those who have been denied entry to the marriage feast of the Lamb despite having been believers in Christ. As friends and loved ones are passed along the way, some of them call out, pleading for me to help them get in, while others bravely shout out congratulations. Weeping bitterly, I move forward with my head down for fear of seeing the look in their eyes, knowing that I have failed them. As the Puritan Nonconformist, Joseph Alleine put it, "Surely, if the lamp of profession would have served the turn, the foolish virgins had never been shut out."[5] Sometimes I feel as Cassandra of

Troy must have felt, she who was both blessed and cursed by the gods--blessed with a gift to accurately foretell the future, cursed in that no one would believe her. And while there have been some who have believed my testimony, there have been many more, especially those dear to me, who have rejected it.

Come, Come, Ye Saints

At the Hill Cumorah Pageant, while getting acquainted with some of the many wonderful young people gathered there, the LDS hymn, "Come, Come Ye Saints," broke out over the loudspeakers. Tears welled up in my eyes, to think that I was a Latter-day Saint. The words of this hymn (which were written by William W. Clayton, 1814-1879) may also be found in any LDS hymnal.

Come, come, ye Saints, no toil nor labor fear;
But with joy wend your way.
Though hard to you this journey may appear,
Grace shall be as your day.
'Tis better far for us to strive
Our useless cares from us to drive;
Do this, and joy your hearts will swell --
All is well! All is well!

Why should we mourn or think our lot is hard?
'Tis not so; all is right.

Why should we think to earn a great reward
If we now shun the fight?
Gird up your loins; fresh courage take.
Our God will never us forsake;
And soon we'll have this tale to tell --
All is well! All is well!

We'll find the place which God for us prepared,
Far away in the West,
Where none shall come to hurt or make afraid;
There the Saints will be blessed.
We'll make the air with music ring,
Shout praises to our God and King;
Above the rest these words we'll tell --
All is well! All is well!

And should we die before our journey's through,
Happy Day! All is well!
We then are free from toil and sorrow, too;
With the just we shall dwell!
But if our lives are spared again
To see the Saints their rest obtain,
Oh, how we'll make this chorus swell --
All is well! All is well!

It's Cold Out There

I attended Ricks College for the Fall semester of 1975. While there, I got to know many young Latter-day Saints, most of whom had been raised in the Church in the western states. I made a lot of good friends. It was a wonderful time in my life. And I was completely smitten with the Mormon girls. I think I fell in love on average about two or three times a month while I was out there. They were amazing: beautiful, spiritual, classy, well-educated, bright-eyed, relationship-minded, and faithful. Yet, notwithstanding the allure of a campus full of Latter-day beauties (one of whom found me imminently kissable), at the end of my first semester--when the icicles started hanging off the buildings at 45 degrees due to the arctic wind--I decided to go home and prepare to serve a mission.

Oh, Maybellene!

Back in Richmond, I was driving the family's orange VW Super Beetle one day, taking a shortcut through the neighborhoods down by the river on my way to the Southside. The road popped out of the trees so close to the foot of the Huguenot Bridge that below the stop sign there was another traffic sign that read, "No Right Turn," i.e., onto the bridge and across the river. Some of us did it anyway because the alternative was to go all the way around on River Road. As I approached the intersection, there was a gap in traffic. I realized that by downshifting into second gear and blowing through the stop sign, my little Beetle would slip right in behind the last car well before the gap closed with no problem. My speed was timed just right, the last car passed me, watching the oncoming cars carefully, I performed the planned maneuver perfectly, only to hit the rear of that last car that, having passed me, had then stopped in the middle of the road at the base of the ramp for no apparent reason. I got out and saw that the damage to both cars was minimal. Then the other driver got out. It was Mabel, who often checked me out of the Safeway grocery store that was just a hundred yards back up the road. I said, "Mabel, why did you stop?" "I knew you weren't going to stop at that stop sign, so I stopped to watch!" "Well, did it not occur to you, knowing as you say that I was not going to stop, that by your stopping in the middle of the road in front of me, our cars would collide?" "Humff," she exclaimed in a high-pitched huff.

When the police got there, Mabel sat in the front seat and I sat in the back of the squad car. The officer, looking at me in the rearview mirror, said, "So tell me, Son, did you come to a complete stop at the stop sign?" "No. But I downshifted into second, does that count?" He had a pretty good idea what had happened, and he was clearly fighting back a smile in the mirror. He asked, "And, which way were you turning?" "Oh, I was turning right." He looked at me again in the mirror, and said, "Well, Son, that's about the most honest thing anyone's ever said in this car. I'm not even going to write you a ticket." "Humff," Mabel exclaimed.

The Firstborn

One morning, having been a member of the Church for a little more than a year, I found myself studying my face in the bathroom mirror. The change in my countenance since joining the Church was truly remarkable. Suddenly, from just down the hall, my brother's voice cried out, "Mother! Mother! Mother!" Something was horribly wrong. He was in a panic. My mother rushed up the stairs, "I'm coming! I'm coming!" Opening the door to his room and finding him lying in bed, she said, "What on earth is wrong?" "There's something sacred about the firstborn!" "What?" "There's something sacred about the firstborn!" She went to his side. "You're my firstborn . . . is that what you mean?" "No, mother. There's something sacred about the firstborn." "What's happened? Tell me what's happened, Son." And then it all came pouring out.

He had gotten his college girlfriend pregnant and she had aborted the child. I watched my face in the mirror as the story unfolded, tears streaming down my cheeks. He was devastated.

I remember thinking that my brother would now be disqualified from serving as a full-time missionary for the Church. It had been mentioned during my baptismal interview that if a young man was involved in a pregnancy that resulted in an abortion, he could not then serve a mission. Since joining the Church, I had always imagined that my brother would be baptized sooner rather than later, and that we would go into the mission field together like Boanerges, sons of thunder. Now, that was not to be.

He did join the Church eventually, about twenty years after I did. I baptized and confirmed him. It was the greatest day of my life. He was an active member for about a year; and then he fell away from the Church. As of this writing, he is a remarkable biblical scholar who considers himself saved by grace, because God wrote his name in the Book of Life before he was born, and nothing else is required. And yet, when Church officials ask him if he wants to remove his name from the LDS membership rolls, he responds, "No. Leave me on the rolls. You never know."

An Unexpected Endorsement

To save up enough money for my LDS mission, I was working for my father making Southern Baptist films. One morning we were having breakfast with the head of the Southern Baptist Convention for South Carolina to discuss the film we were shooting about their mission work among the migrant field workers in the state. This good Baptist brother innocently asked, "So, Sean, what are your plans?" "I'm saving money to go on a Mormon mission." You talk about your lead balloon. To my surprise, my father jumped in, "Say what you will about the Mormons, they have done for my son what my church either wouldn't, or couldn't do." By which he meant, straighten me out, having witnessed the transformation I had undergone since my baptism.

Missionary Farewell

Sometime around April of 1976, I received my mission call to the Anaheim, California, Spanish-speaking Mission. As was the custom at that time, one whole Sacrament meeting was devoted to my farewell. I got to organize the program, selecting the hymns to be sung, etc.; and I was to be the main speaker.

Now, back then our chapels weren't furnished with one of those demure, little, black miniature marshmallows at the end of a thin flexible wand that passes for a microphone these days. No, back in the day, it was a hardy steel tube with a full-sized cardioid hand mic attached to the end by a plastic clip, all tentatively held in place by a single wingnut at the base. I began with, "It will probably be a while before you forget my last talk . . ." Just then the wingnut gave way. The entire microphone assemblage fell forward, slammed into my chest and slid down my tie where it landed in the vicinity of my belt buckle with an audible thud. (I take this as proof positive that God has a sense of humor.) Making no other movement, I looked down at the microphone. There was some nervous laughter in the chapel. A member of the Bishopric came up from behind me, hoisted the three pounds of steel and plastic back into place, tightened the wing nut, and then whispered to me, "OK, go ahead." I continued, "And I suppose it will be a while before you forget this one." The laughter was way too loud for a Sacrament meeting. Fortunately, though, this time I had prepared, proving that I can be taught. Once under way, my talk took on a more somber tone. As I bore my testimony of the restored gospel, I turned to face my parents and my sister who were seated to one side, behind me on the dais. They were weeping like children. And so, I said farewell to my family and to the Latter-day Saints in Richmond, Virginia, whom I had grown to love. A few days later, I boarded a plane for Utah where I was to spend the next two months learning how to preach the restored gospel, and to speak Spanish, among other things.

The Mission

"Seek not to declare my word, but first seek to obtain my word, and then shall your tongue be loosed; then, if you desire, you shall have my Spirit and my word, yea, the power of God unto the convincing of men." (Doctrine and Covenants 11:21)

Onward and Upward

At the missionary training center (MTC) in Provo, Utah we studied Spanish grammar and vocabulary; and we memorized key scriptures and missionary lessons in Spanish. My roommate told me that I sat bolt upright in my bunk bed one night and recited one of the lessons in Spanish perfectly. Of course, the next day in class, I made a hash of it again. I'll never forget the Elders in my group at the MTC: Big Al from Chicago, McMurtrey, Goodall, and Kirby, to name a few.

My first day in California, I met my Mission President, Rex C. Reeve Sr., and my first companion, Elder Merrill Nelson. He was from Grantsville, Utah, and was selected to be my trainer. There was the possibility of my being assigned to work with any one of several Elders who were present that day. But when Elder Nelson bore his testimony during our meeting, there was a visible light coming from his eyes, and I remember thinking, "I hope I get him." In retrospect, he was the finest missionary I ever saw in the field.

I taught my first lesson in English. Our investigator was a

young man named Rudy that Elder Nelson and his previous companion had been teaching. After covering two lessons that evening--at my companion's prompting--I invited Rudy to be baptized. He accepted without reservation. I was off to a good start. The first lesson I taught in Spanish, however, reduced me to tears as I realized that the family we were teaching didn't understand what I was saying. As we left, their little girl turned on the sprinklers and soaked me from the waist down.

After I adjusted to missionary life, and my Spanish improved a little, Elder Nelson and I began to meet with more consistent success, which continued for me long after he had returned home. He only had about six months left on his mission when he was assigned to show me the ropes. In all, over the two years I was a full-time missionary, I taught hundreds of people from almost every Spanish-speaking country in Central and South America, including Cuba. Of that number, approximately 30 to 40 people were baptized into the Church while I was still on my mission. I didn't keep an accurate count. This approximate number does not include those who were too young to be baptized with their parents, nor those who took longer to gain a testimony of the restored gospel, and were baptized after I had left the mission field. As the cliché goes, the mission years were literally the best two years of my life. When it was over, I didn't want to go home.

Most of the highly spiritual moments of religious conversion in those we taught would be better related by them. We were only witness to a small portion of the process. Though we were privileged to play a role in their conversions, trying to relate their experiences from our limited perspective really wouldn't do them justice; you had to be the one experiencing it. In short, the humble seekers of truth that we encountered dreamed dreams, had their faithful prayers answered, wept as we taught them the restored gospel, placed their hands over their hearts and repeated their variation of the words Mike had spoken to me in that jeep. We frequently witnessed miracles as their lives were changed and they overcame the world with God's help. Suffice it to say that the Spirit of God bore powerful witness to the truthfulness of the restored gospel. And those who had ears to hear received that witness and accepted our invitation to follow the Savior into the waters of baptism.

We were actively engaged in missionary work six days out of every week. Mondays, however, were set aside for taking care of everything else: laundry, shopping, letter writing, and often some sort of recreational activity. We referred to Monday as "preparation day," or "p-day" for short. The following accounts touch on some of the people we encountered, a few of those we taught and baptized, one or two of the members of the Church we met, and some of the more entertaining experiences that occurred on p-days.

Thanks!

One day I was assigned to work with Elder Bradley for the afternoon (on occasion four Elders would get together and exchange companions, or "split up"). He was an English-speaking Elder, so we were on his turf knocking on doors in a neighborhood of multi-million-dollar tract houses. We approached a large mansion that looked to be situated on a full acre of perfectly maintained lawn. There was a long walkway that meandered toward the front door. As we opened the gate of the picket fence and stepped off the sidewalk onto the path, the front door opened abruptly. A man emerged from the house moving at an alarming pace. He was built like a fullback and coming right at us. We met about a third of the way to the house, where he suddenly stopped directly in front of us at arm's length. Looking us in the eyes, he said, "Mormons?" "Yes, sir." He sized us up, spotted a copy of the Book of Mormon in Elder Bradley's hand and said, "Book of Mormon?" "Yes, sir." He then reached out, snatched the book from Elder Bradley's hand and held it up at eye level, saying, "Thanks! I've been wanting one of these." And with that, he turned on his heels and headed back toward the front door at the same pace he had come through it. I don't remember what Elder Bradley called after him; but the man just raised the book over his head, and without turning around said something like, "I'll get back to you." The door closed behind him, and that was that. I'm sure Elder Bradley followed up with him, but I don't think I ever heard how that played out.

[As a completely gratuitous aside, several years later, while I was a student at BYU, I had a chance encounter with Elder Bradley, but the subject didn't come up. I was windsurfing on Deer Creek Reservoir, which is up the canyon from Provo. It's a great spot with very consistent winds in the afternoons; and the wind was really blowing that day. I was moving over the water at around 15 knots when I spotted another windsurfer, on nearly a collision course, cutting across my bow at the same speed. Neither one of us slowed down, and as we closely passed one another, I got a good look at the other guy. He looked a lot like Elder Bradley. I said, "Bradley, is that you?" Looking back over his shoulder, "Stewart?" "Yeah." "Hey!" As the wind swept us apart, we either agreed or assumed that we would meet up on the beach later. But it's a big body of water and there were quite a few sails out there that day. I lost track of him, and haven't seen him since. It wasn't a reunion like Forrest Gump and Lt. Dan; but I enjoyed it.]

Not to Worry

And then there was the time Elder Nelson and I were knocking on doors and found a Portuguese family that had a vineyard in their backyard. Only the elderly father and his adult daughter were home. They invited us in for a chat and offered us some wine, which we politely declined, of course. After a few minutes of conversation, the father, who spoke more Portuguese than English, left the room to attend to something; so we carried on with the daughter who spoke perfect English. I explained that while wine was taboo, we could sample their grape juice if they had any. She took a container from the fridge and filled a couple of tall glasses. I took one sip and, having quaffed a beaker or two in my youth, knew immediately that we had been served an alcoholic beverage. Elder Nelson took a sip and seemed to enjoy it. In his defense, having been raised in a Mormon home, I doubt he had ever tasted alcohol in his life. Compounding the matter was the fact that he lacked the sense of smell, which severely curtails one's ability to taste. While the daughter returned the container to the fridge, I set my glass down and told my companion that I had tasted alcohol. He said, "Oh no, they wouldn't do that to us." Then he continued to drink his "juice." The conversation progressed until the father returned. I asked him about the container in the fridge, "What percent alcohol would that be?" "Oh, not to worry, no more than four or five percent." The daughter agreed. So, we found out the hard way what passed for grape juice in their family.

As we took our leave, Elder Nelson had a rosy glow about him. And I'd like to think we did some of our best work later that afternoon. Unfortunately, though, I really don't remember what we did later that afternoon; and I know Merrill doesn't remember. I mean, let's face it, for a Mormon missionary, he was hitting the sauce pretty hard back in those days. I'm fond of saying that, later in life, he was elected to public office in Utah only because I failed to come forward.

Then the Full Corn Shall Appear

All the Elders in our zone were playing touch football one p-day. Elder Nelson and I were switching off at quarterback on our team. My companion had played quarterback on his high school football team. I just happened to have a good arm and a tight spiral from years of backyard pickup games. It was my turn; and as it was getting late, we decided that the next touchdown would win. Also on our team was Elder

Corn. I could never forget his name because it was around Thanksgiving, and when we sang the hymn that goes, "First the blade and then the ear, then the full corn shall appear," he smiled and we exchanged a knowing glance. He was a very personable young man with a luminous, if imperfect smile, who reminded one of John Ritter somehow. He was also one of the least coordinated individuals I had ever met. It was 50/50 he would catch a football if you lobbed it to him underhand from a few yards away. For that reason, Elder Corn had not touched the ball the entire game. He would stand on the line, and when the ball was snapped, he would just mill around until the play was over. No one ever blocked him on defense, and no one ever covered him on offense. He was strictly ornamental.

We had about fifteen yards to go, and it occurred to me that if Elder Corn could somehow catch the ball in the end zone, we would win the game. So, in the huddle I called for Elder Corn to line up on the center's right and everyone else to line up to the right of Elder Corn, leaving the left side of the line wide-open. On the snap, everyone but Elder Corn was to run a diagonal pattern into the left corner of the end zone, taking all the coverage with them. Elder Corn was to then go to the right corner of the end zone, where he would be wide-open, catch the ball and win the game. Elder Corn couldn't believe what he was hearing, and he wasn't the only one in the huddle in disbelief. He said, "No, don't throw the ball to me. I'll drop it." Something I had read in *The Inner Game of Tennis* sprang to mind. I said, "Elder, the only reason you can't catch a football is, no one has ever told you the secret. There's a trick to it, anyone can do it." "Really?" Disbelief gave way to cautiously optimistic concern in the huddle as the other Elders wondered where this was going. We all felt bad about his being left out of every play; and it was obvious that he wanted to do something to help the team. In his eyes, though, was clearly written a long history of failure where any kind of sport was concerned. His fear of being the goat again was palpable. I said, "Yeah, all you have to do is concentrate on which way the ball is spinning so your hands are ready for that little twist when you catch it. Otherwise, it twists out of your hands because you didn't pay attention to which way it was spinning. That's all there is to it." Elder Corn looked around the huddle and got reassuring words and glances from the Elders. He said, "All right, if you think it'll work." "We can't miss, no one's covered you all day. Just concentrate on the spin."

Like Gawaine le Cœur-Hardy armed with his magic word, Elder Corn took his place on the line. The ball was snapped. The rush poured across the empty left side of the line. Everyone else on the field ran to the left corner of the end zone, except for Elder Corn and me. I rolled out to the right to evade the rush. Elder Corn jogged to the right corner of the end zone, turned to face me, and planted his feet. No one was within 15 yards of him. I released a nice spiral, and in my defense, the ball left my hand with a little more heat on it than I had intended. Elder Corn appeared to be in a trance as he focused on the spinning ball. As it got closer to him, his eyes seemed to cross from the intense concentration. It looked like it was going to hit him in the forehead. I winced, thinking I may have just broken his nose. Then, just before the ball smashed into his face, he put his hands up . . . to block it, or to grab it; we'll never know. Anyway, when he came to, and realized that he was standing in the end zone with the ball in his hands, he lit up like a Christmas tree. There was a lot of backslapping and attaboys on our side, while the other team grumbled, "Corn! I can't believe it." In retrospect, he probably caught the ball out of an instinct for self-preservation; but it didn't matter. For the first time in his life Elder Corn had caught a football for a touchdown--to win the game.

Snapshots of Missionary Life

No two days were the same. We never knew when we stepped out the front door what was waiting for us out there. One day, Elder Nelson and I were knocking on doors, when we spotted a young boy, maybe five or six years old, who stopped us in our tracks. He was wearing an adult-size batter's helmet backwards and trying to push a tiny bike with training wheels across the lawn while carrying his shoes. Every two or three feet, he would drop a shoe, then pick it up and start over. He was shaped like an egg, and had one of those faces that was just comedic. We laughed until tears filled our eyes watching him. Then he looked up at us with an expression that said, "What's so funny?" We went over and got to know him. His name was Benny. Elder Nelson threw the ball and Benny took a few swings for us. He was definitely a power hitter in the making, a modern-day "bambino."

One hot summer day, three of us were knocking on doors together, and we got a little punchy. Elder Nelson, Elder Olsen and I were there. We decided to spruce up our door approach a little. One of us would step forward and speak our usual introductory lines to whomever opened a door, while the other two would stand a step behind and softly sing a little doo-wop in the background. One lady opened her door, and then leaned a little closer to make sure she was really hearing what she thought she was hearing. It went something like this: Bah Bohm, Bah Bohm, "Hello Ma'am," Ba Bohm Bah Bah Bah Bah Bohm "We represent the Church . . ." and repeat.

Another Elder and I arrived for a teaching appointment one afternoon to find our young, very attractive female investigator wearing a skimpy halter top and blue jeans that were cut off so short they didn't cover the pockets. We taught the first lesson like that. Afterwards, I explained to my companion (who wasn't completely committed to "the program" at that point) that the next time we were going to skip to the final lesson which covered modesty in dress. He was incensed, "You can't do that! We have to teach the lessons in order." "No, I'm not doing that again." For our next visit, she was dressed about the same, and as we covered the topic of modesty in dress, she looked a little hurt and asked if she should go change. I said, "It might be best." When she came back down the stairs--wearing an additional ten or twelve square inches of material--and asked if that was better, my companion grinned like the Cheshire cat, and I said, "Yeah, thanks."

What Did You Say?

By way of background, I should explain here that the typical experience of the Spanish-speaking Elders was quite a bit different from that of the English-speaking Elders in Southern California. The latter had more doors slammed in their faces than we did. They also seemed to have a more difficult time fomenting a spiritual experience among their investigators. Elder Olsen and I, on the other hand, would come back to the apartment we shared with two English-speaking Elders, open the door and say in unison, "Thar's gold in them thar hills!" To which they would jovially reply, "Yeah, yeah, pipe down." Then we would share with them stories of people bursting into tears because the Spirit was so strong in the room while we were teaching them. The Latinos would have dreams about us before we ever knocked on their doors. Case in point, as we were driving one Latino sister to her baptism at the stake center, where she never had been before, as we turned the last corner she cried out, "That is the building I saw in my dream!"

So, against that backdrop, one day the phone rang in the apartment. On the other end was one Mr. Gallardo. He said that he and his family had seen the Osmonds on TV, and they wanted to be baptized so they could be like the Osmonds. He wanted to know if their baptisms could be arranged. It was explained to him that that wouldn't be a problem, and an appointment was set for their first lesson. We were to teach them in English, as they were completely Anglicized. When we walked into their home, Mr. and Mrs. Gallardo and their four beautiful children were dressed in their Sunday best, sitting on the sofa with their hands folded, waiting for us to teach them.

And so it went for the first three or four lessons. Then it was time to explain the law of tithing, in accordance with which members give 10% of their income to the Church. As soon as the words reverberated off the walls, the father interrupted us, "I'm sorry, what did you say?" We went through it again, and he said, "No! That's not possible. You must leave." We tried to explain the blessings that came from paying tithing; but he would have none of it. He was done, adding only, "I'm sorry, but you must go. Now, please!" We found ourselves standing outside on the porch as the door closed behind us, thinking, "What just happened?" Apparently, we had been sucked in by fool's gold.

The Angels

I met Lou and Ann Stokes, who were members of the Church, when they had my companion and me over for dinner one night. Their young daughter, whom they had late in life and named Louann, was also present. Lou mentioned that he had box seats to the Angels' games at Anaheim Stadium; and he invited us to watch a game on our p-day. We happily accepted; and a few days later as we were enjoying America's pastime, Lou told us the following story. One day he's watching a game when the Spirit whispers to him to go call his wife. This is well before cell phones, and he can't think of any reason why he would need to call his wife, so he ignores the prompting. Again, the Spirit urges him to call his wife. So, he gets up and makes the long trek to the payphone. His wife says everything is fine. He hangs up the phone and starts back to his seat thinking, "What was that all about?" When he finally gets back, the guy in the next box over says, "Hey Lou, you missed it. While you were gone, this guy smacked a line drive, hit your seat right in the numbers." Lou had a pacemaker.

When the Dog Bites

My companion and I had joined forces with two English-speaking Elders with the intention of splitting up. I was to spend the day working with Elder Atine, who was a full-blooded Navajo. Elder Atine was about 30 yards in front of me as we pedaled our bicycles to a teaching appointment. We were rolling along a quiet residential street that had a bright rose-colored stucco wall running almost the entire length of the block. Between the wall and the street was a sidewalk. Sticking out of the sidewalk was a utility pole. And crouched behind the pole, unseen by me, there was a very stealthy bulldog lying in wait. As I came alongside the pole, I saw movement out of the corner of my right eye. Suddenly--and this is the only time in my life this has happened--everything around me went into slow motion, literally.

I looked down and saw a mostly white bulldog seemingly suspended in midair. He had lunged at me from his hiding place. I had all the time in the world to analyze the scene. Judging from his trajectory, he was apparently anticipating that my right foot would come down with the pedal on the next stroke. His plan was to sink his teeth into my ankle at the bottom of that stroke. His jaws slowly gaped wider as he inched closer to his mark. His teeth were exposed, and there was drool hanging from his jowls that were flapping around his snout in slow motion. The tips of my shoes were clipped into the pedals; but, as my right foot came to the top of the fateful stroke, I pulled my shoe free and lifted my right knee up and to the left. My other foot pulled up on the left pedal, which forced my right pedal to drop down, footless. I leaned out a little to the right to get a good look. No doubt he had perfected this move over many dog years, and he knew that he had timed it just right. He was a master of his craft. I watched his jaws close shut on nothing but air, just above the pedal. And then, as if someone had thrown a switch, the light went out of his eyes. I've never seen disappointment and disbelief so clearly expressed on an animal's face. As my right pedal returned to the top, the whole scene came back up to normal speed. The dog barked a few times and gave chase as far as his fat little legs would carry him, which was about five yards. Elder Atine heard the barking and looked over his shoulder at me. I caught up to him and we pedaled on to our meeting unmolested.

I Used to Have Power

As an interesting aside, during my entire two-year mission, I only recall totally blowing off two hours or so when I should have been doing missionary work. We were splitting up again, and our companions had already left, when suddenly a water fight broke out between myself and Elder Atine. For some reason, there were a couple of squirt guns and some balloons in their apartment. It escalated pretty quickly, and before we knew what had happened, it was out of control. I was basically getting shellacked. At one point, while charging around a corner with my squirt gun blazing, a water balloon exploded in the middle of my back. I don't know if being Navajo gave him an edge, but Elder Atine had mad skillz. Suddenly, we realized that our companions were returning to the apartment. They asked us how our morning had gone. Since I was soaking wet, and Elder Atine was slightly damp, we had to sheepishly confess that we had never actually made it out of the apartment complex.

A Letter from Home

I corresponded with my family on a fairly regular basis throughout my mission. My Father once told me that reading my letters was one of the spiritual highlights of his life. One day a letter came from my mother concerning a neighbor who hadn't crossed my mind in years. First, a little background.

All the way up through high school, my mother was known to my friends in the neighborhood as Sherlock--Sherls or Sherly for short--because we could never put anything over on her. My brother and I were constantly getting busted, while our friends, who were equally guilty, went scot-free. We used to joke that she kept files on all of us. To this day, friends from my youth will inquire, "How's Sherls doing?" So, now you know who we are dealing with.

Sometime around the age of seven or eight, I had a friend in the neighborhood named Eric. One day, while at his house, his father said, "Boys, I'll give you a quarter for every bag of apples you bring me from Mrs. Smith's orchard." This was to be done without Mrs. Smith's knowledge or permission. The orchard was directly behind their property and only protected by a hedge. We managed to purloin two bags of apples, for which we were each paid 25 cents. When I got home and proudly displayed my quarter, my mother asked me where I had gotten it. Upon hearing my story, she said, "Go get in the car." She then drove me to Mrs. Smith's house and marched me up to the front door, having explained to me that I was to ring the bell, tell Mrs. Smith what I had done, and give her the quarter. The elderly, grey-haired woman heard my confession, and then, when I offered her the quarter, said, "Oh, that's all right, you can keep it." I looked up at my mom who was shooting Mrs. Smith a death ray stare which clearly communicated that it was **not** all right, and that she **would** be taking the quarter--which she did.

To put the finishing touches on that lesson about honesty, the letter I received from my mother in the mission field contained a newspaper clipping. My childhood friend's father had been arrested by the FBI in Chicago for embezzling funds from his employer. And that is how Sherly finally closed that case, after working it for twelve years.

The Boys

We got a referral on a Filipino family that we started teaching. The parents were interested, but their three sons were golden. They were about 8, 10, and 12 years old: Jamey, Junior, and Bobby. They took to the lessons like three little sponges, always happy and enthusiastic to learn more about the restored gospel. When we invited the family to be baptized, the mother and father were hesitant, but the boys accepted immediately. With their parent's permission, all three boys were baptized and confirmed members of the Church. After seeing the effect that membership in the Church had on their sons, the mother and father were baptized about three weeks later. We got to know the family pretty well. They invited us to their home for dinner one Christmas Eve. When we meet again, if I find out that Jamey, Junior, and Bobby did not all three grow up to serve full-time missions, I'll be stunned.

Be Healed

We were teaching a Mexican couple with an infant child; they were probably undocumented. During one visit, they told us how deeply troubled they were because the child was very ill. We explained what a priesthood blessing was; and they asked us to bless their child. We laid our hands on the sleeping infant, and Elder Smith anointed the baby's head with consecrated oil. I sealed the anointing and pronounced a blessing, during which I said, "Sea sanado," which is in English, "Be healed." As the words left my mouth, the tiny body beneath our hands convulsed one time, and then the baby continued to sleep peacefully. The next time we visited them the baby was happy and healthy; but the parents were no longer interested in continuing their study of the Church. They attributed the baby's sudden recovery to some medicine they had gotten their hands on from a "doctor" in Tijuana.

Dead Man's Turn

One p-day, some members of the Church put our bicycles into a pickup truck, loaded about 12 of us into a caravan of cars, and took us nearly to the top of one peak in the Santa Ana Mountains. The plan was to ride our bikes down the mountain, and then they would pick us up at the bottom. Most of us had never done this before, but it sounded like fun. At the top there was a rustic convenience store of sorts where we congregated before getting started. An elderly man was sitting alone in the corner by a Franklin stove. He asked, "Are you boys riding down the mountain?" "Yes, sir." "Well, you keep a sharp eye out for dead man's turn." We assured him that we would; but no one really took him seriously. Once we were out of earshot, Elder Atine, with a gleam in his eye, responded for my benefit, "OK, Pops."

As we barreled down the mountain we were reaching speeds of 45 mph or so. At one point, Elder Brower was drafting me closely in an attempt to coax a little more speed out of his ride. His front tire was maybe three or four feet from my back tire. I was staying low, having become one with my machine, 18 pounds of highly-tuned Shimano. Elder Brower was perched atop 30 pounds of rusting Schwinn. After looking over my shoulder to see how close he was, I looked forward again and realized that dead man's turn was upon us. It was a brutal hairpin that we were going way too fast to hold. I sat up and hit both brakes hard. Elder Brower, seeing my reaction, also hit his brakes, but they just sagged. He later said his bike seemed to go faster. He had one split second to make a choice. He could keep straight and slam into the back of my bike. Or, he could go left into possible oncoming traffic. Or, he could go right toward a guard rail that overlooked a thousand-foot drop to certain death. Elder Brower, good Mormon boy that he was, had to "choose the right."

I was unaware of his predicament until I heard a strange clicking noise and looked over to see him sliding along the guardrail, where some part of his bike was hitting every bolt as he went. Directly in front of him was a small sign that read, "No stopping, standing, or parking." His front tire wedged between the sign post and the guardrail, causing his bike to come to an abrupt halt. Elder Brower was now airborne. Of course, the laws of physics decreed that he should have flown over the guardrail and landed 1000 feet below. Instead, he somehow ended up in the middle of the lane, flat on his back with barely a scratch on him.

When I reached him, he was staring straight up at me and seemed to be talking, but he wasn't making any sound. Then I realized he wasn't breathing. He'd had the wind knocked out of him. As the other Elders who had been behind us gathered around, I said, "Come on, Elder, breathe!" He just stared at us with his mouth wide-open and a chagrined look on his face. Suddenly he sucked in a deep breath, looked right at me, and said in a hoarse whisper, "Why did you stop?" Apparently, Elder Brower thought that maintaining speed and leaning into dead man's turn was the way to go. But then, he was a downhill racer from Sun Valley, Idaho; so that could explain it.

Wackadoodles

If you go around knocking on doors long enough, you're bound to run into some serious wackadoodles. Yeah, they're out there. There were the typical wackadoodles, like the one man who wore a tinfoil hat and had tinfoil on the windows so the government couldn't read his thoughts. And then there were the legendary wackadoodles: One Elder told me that he had a woman open the door completely naked (and this was California, not Denmark where that kind of thing happens all the time). But the winner of the wackadoodle award has to go to a woman we were teaching in Spanish one day. I was reading aloud from the Old Testament concerning Moses and something that had happened, when suddenly she interrupted me, saying, "No. That is not what happened. I saw the movie! What happened was . . ." And then she explained it to me, a la Cecil B. DeMille, chapter and verse. I didn't know where to go from there.

Something Was Off

We were teaching a young, attractive woman one evening who lived alone in a townhouse. This was our second or third lesson. Suddenly, to my surprise, a key was heard working the lock at the front door, which opened. A man entered. The woman we were teaching didn't seem surprised or alarmed, and yet, something was off. Even though he was standing directly under a light in the foyer, I couldn't make out his features. There seemed to be a dark cloud hovering over him. It was eerie. He came closer and, without much of an introduction, sat down next to our investigator. He then explained that he was a member of the Church, and that he was in a temple marriage with children. He also confessed that he was having an affair with our investigator. This was apparently the reason she had taken an interest in the Church. As he attempted to justify what he was doing, I asked him if he was happy. He said, "Yes." She quickly interjected, "But you told me you weren't." He just looked at her pleadingly. We could not, of course, continue teaching her under the circumstances; so, we said our goodbyes.

The King of Hawaii

My companion at the time was Elder Galloway, who was in California waiting for a visa to Brazil. I don't recall where he got the thing (possibly from Elder Brower), but he had an old Schwinn that he loved to tinker with. He would break it down on p-days, oil it, polish it, and then put it back together. One p-day, after his ritual was completed, we pedaled off to play racquetball somewhere in Anaheim. Our route took us down a road along a railroad track that had stop signs at the end of each block for about a quarter mile. Every time we went this way, we would race up to each stop sign, slam on the brakes, come to a complete stop (even though there was rarely any traffic) and then, balancing so that no time was wasted by putting a foot on the ground, we would start to pedal again. On this day, as we rapidly approached the first stop sign, Elder Galloway slammed on his brakes, but only the front brake grabbed. He went over the handlebars, and being reluctant to let go of them, did a face-plant with his rear tire sticking straight up in the air. Having ascertained that he wasn't seriously injured, I said, "Elder, if you can repeat that, you can earn a living." He tried to force a smile, but winced, as the road rash on one side of his face was pretty bad.

The next day, we were knocking on doors in Cypress, when we met this five-foot-something tree trunk of a man who was Hawaiian. He said he was a member of the Church. He was about twice as tall as he was wide, and one of his eyes looked like a marble, in that, where you would normally see an iris, all the colors were mixed together. He was obviously blind in that eye. When we told him what had happened to Elder Galloway's face, he went into his front yard and picked some leaves off of an aloe Vera plant growing there. He snapped one in two and applied the gel to my companion's road rash. Then he gave him the extra leaves and prescribed several applications a day. It worked; when the abrasion eventually healed, there was no trace of a scar.

The man introduced himself as brother Nuuhiwa. I recognized the last name as that of a professional surfer I had followed in surfing magazines back in the day. The famous surfer turned out to be his son. We learned he also had a daughter who was a high-wire acrobat with Ringling Brothers. And he spoke of a younger daughter that everyone was watching with great anticipation. He invited us into his house through the garage where we stood around getting to know him. We learned that he was one of the world's foremost experts in the martial arts. I don't remember what style he practiced, I believe it came from China, but he had been awarded the red belt signifying the level of master, which is far above a black belt. He said only three Americans had ever received it. Then he started warming up so he could put his fist through a board for us. This consisted of placing his hand on the cement floor and bouncing a ball-peen hammer off his knuckles repeatedly and with gusto. As he did that, he told us about the time he was giving a demonstration at a luncheon, and while he was working over his knuckles with the hammer, a lady in the front row had thrown up. It took both of us to hold the board so he could break it.

I noticed a mounted newspaper clipping on the wall. It described an appearance by our host on a television show back in the 50's called, *You Asked for It.* The premise was that people would write in asking to see something, and the producers would try to make it happen. Well, someone had written in asking to see a man kill a bull with his bare hands. (Can you imagine the hellfire that PETA would rain down on a show like that today?) Somehow they found brother Nuuhiwa, who accepted the challenge. He told us how he had studied the bull's cranial structure and determined that the right amount of pressure from a firm blow at the right point coming from above would cave in the animal's skull. The article described brother Nuuhiwa walking into the field where the bull was kept as the cameras rolled. I read aloud that as he drew closer to the bull, it suddenly charged. At this point, he said, "Yeah, I wasn't expecting that." Then, as the bull was about to gore him, he took an agile step to one side, and rapped the animal on the head with a closed fist as it went by. All four legs came out from under it, and the bull went down at his feet. I never saw the footage, but that's how the newspaper article described it.

After that he talked about the good old days when he had fought in a league of martial artists who went at it with no rules until someone was disabled. This was illegal in the United States, so the fights were always held in some far-flung corner of the globe. He told us about one fight he had in Africa with a seven-foot-tall Watusi warrior. It seems the big man had caved in brother Nuuhiwa ribs with a long-range roundhouse kick. But he absorbed the blow, and was able to work his way inside where he ripped out the Watusi's trachea with his index finger. Apparently, this was his signature move. Because they were in the middle of nowhere, the Watusi died before he could receive much-needed medical attention. I asked him how he felt about that, in light of the Church's teachings concerning the shedding of innocent blood. He said he wasn't a member of the Church back then, and besides, they all knew what they were signing up for.

I inquired about his eye. He told us that he had lost it in a fight while he was going for the trachea of a Chinese master. He managed to get it, but in the process his opponent had scrambled his eye. It seems no one died that day, but that was the end of his fighting career. Even so, the local SWAT team had used him once in a hostage situation. They sent in this short, harmless looking Hawaiian guy with one eye, the next thing they knew it was all over and the hostages were coming out. I was just glad he was on our side.

He said there had been a vote on the islands and he had

been awarded the honorary title of "King of Hawaii" because of his royal blood. There was a picture of him placing a lei around the neck of the winner of the Waimea Canoe Race. They would fly him over there a couple times a year for various ceremonies. He was a living legend.

Feliz Navidad

We were teaching a large Mexican family who were in the country illegally. The husband and wife with their six children were living in a two-bedroom cinderblock hut. We were teaching them one evening when my eye was drawn to the ceiling which seemed to be moving. It was crawling with flies. The mother cooked "mole" (pronounced "MOH-lay," a Mexican dish that does not include moles) for us one day as we watched; it was her specialty. She started by taking a chunk of lard the size of a goat's head and throwing it into a pot. I'd like to think I ate it, and enjoyed it; but all I know for sure is, I really wished I hadn't seen how it was made. The only name I recall is that of their youngest son, Danny, who was running around the place in diapers.

One day in December, when we came for a visit, the father was in a cast; he had broken his arm on a construction site where he was a laborer. As a result, he couldn't work; and when he didn't work, he didn't get paid. There was no worker's compensation because of his illegal status. It became apparent to us that they had no money to celebrate Christmas that year. Their home was situated in a forgotten corner of a ward that consisted mainly of wealthy members of the Church. When we told the ward leadership about this family, they took up a collection of toys, clothes and food. We were entrusted with getting it all to the family before Christmas. Early on Christmas Eve we piled it all up against the front door, knocked loudly, and then ran across the street to hide behind a large tree. As we watched from afar, the door opened; we could hear the children shouting with glee. After they loaded it all into the house, one of the older girls started looking around and spotted us. Being discovered, we came out of hiding and wished them a Feliz Navidad.

America's Guru

At one point, we were teaching a beautiful, single Latino woman named America. Her house was like an international hostel; she always seemed to have houseguests, and they were from all over the world. I don't recall how she met all these people. One day she had us over for dinner, along with a swami from India, a few of his local devotees, and a couple of Indian Ph.D.s, who were husband and wife. When we arrived, someone opened the door, and we had to introduce ourselves to the guru, who was known to all as Swami Ji. After a minute or two of conversation, America came into the room and said, "Ah, Swami, I see you've met my Elder friends." Swami stood and walked out of the room, saying, "Yes, and I am already bored with them."

We were all seated at the long, formal dining room table. About ten minutes into the meal, Swami looked heavenward and began to recite something in Hindi that sounded like a prayer. I put down my fork and looked at America. She said, "He does this all the time, just keep eating." When Swami rejoined us, I asked, "So tell me, Swami, what's life like for a swami in India?" The two Ph.D.s seated across from me shared a barely perceptible snicker. Swami launched into a lengthy response that may or may not have included the one memorable pearl of wisdom he shared with us, which was also written down in a pamphlet he gave us and went like this: "Light and sound current is [sic] the absolute Generator, Operator, Destroyer of the universe, giver of happiness, health and harmony to the personkind. It is [sic] ultimate cause and source of it all." He went on to tell us that when he was six years old, he had achieved cosmic consciousness, at which point he knew all things. I asked him if that meant he knew my birthday. He chuckled softly and said, "No, my son, I know all things, but I am constantly rediscovering them." "So, if I told you my birthday, you would have rediscovered what you already knew?" "Yes, that's correct." The devotees didn't seem put off by Swami's ramblings; but at some point the Ph.D.s couldn't take it anymore. The husband weighed in, "You want to know what a swami does in India? He wanders the countryside offering himself to the ladies. He's basically a gigolo." I thought the devotee seated to my side was going to have a stroke.

After dinner, we were looking pretty good to Swami compared to the Ph.D.s. He showed us his photo album which contained pictures of him with everyone who was anyone in Indian politics, save Mahatma Gandhi only. Nehru, Indira Gandhi . . . they were all in there standing next to a much younger Swami Ji, smiling and shaking hands. He was the real deal. His followers were building him a temple in Southern California. When it came time to leave, Swami said to me, "Tell your people to come to me. I will show them the way." "Ah, sorry Swami, that job's already taken." He smiled, gave us a little namaste bow, and we parted in peace.

Gloria in Excelsis Deo

One day we were knocking our way through a barrio when a young Mexican woman opened the door. There was visible light shining from her eyes in the dimly-lit hallway. She had the most angelic face I had ever seen, very much like Olivia Hussey, the actress chosen to portray Juliet and the mother of Christ in films because of the striking purity of her countenance. Her name was Gloria. We began teaching her, her husband, Saul, their young son, Saul, Jr., and her brother-in-law, Raul. She spoke very little English; but we walked into an English-speaking Sacrament meeting one Sunday and found her sitting alone at the back of the Chapel. She didn't understand what was being said. She was just there to feel the Spirit. We sat down beside her and started translating. There was a wonderful spirit in their home as well, as they befriended us and we testified of the truthfulness of the restored gospel. Raul, the brother-in-law, was baptized on Christmas Eve, 1977. Gloria was baptized on Jan. 28th, 1978. Saul, Jr. had to wait a few months to be of age, and Saul, Sr., wasn't ready. Eventually, Gloria's brother and sister were also baptized. My journal records the following:

"May 6, 1978: Today, Jose Luis and Guillermina [Gloria's brother and sister] were baptized. Elder Mobley baptized him, and I baptized her and confirmed them. Sister Tallabas was there, she's the grandmother of the Tallabas clan. She said she wanted to be baptized."

"May 10, 1978: Today is Guillermina's 15th birthday. We went by to celebrate her Quinceañera with the family, who are all baptized now except for Saul, Sr. Three of them, Gloria, Jose Luis, and Guillermina are from Jalisco; and their mother, who is Catholic, doesn't know they have converted."

Several years later at BYU, I met a young man who had just recently returned from my old mission field. I asked him if he had happened to meet Gloria and her family while he was there. He said, "Yes, I baptized the father, Saul." That's going to be a happy reunion someday, when I see that beautiful family again, together forever.

As I Have Loved You, Love One Another

My mission president, Rex C. Reeve Sr., was called to be a member of the First Quorum of Seventy while he was yet serving the last few months of his mission. He flew up to Salt Lake City for General Conference to be sustained. When he returned, he told us that President Spencer W. Kimball had greeted him at the airport, kissed him on the cheek and said, "I've waited three days to tell you I love you."

Upon hearing this, I was reminded of a young adult conference in Virginia Beach that I had attended as a recent convert. Elder David B. Haight was there to speak to us, only a few hours after being called to the Quorum of the Twelve Apostles. His visit there constituted his first public appearance as an apostle. He was in tears as he related to us how President Kimball had extended the call to him, saying, "With all the love I possess, I am calling you to fill the vacancy in the Quorum of the Twelve Apostles."

I don't recall ever feeling more loved than when I was in the presence of my mission president. The man **was** love. Serving as one of his missionaries was the greatest privilege of my life. I gained an inkling into what it would have been like to have such a man for a father. My respect for him is boundless to this day. I asked him once how I was doing, just in general, as a member of the Church. He looked at me with his kind, wise eyes and said, "Elder Stewart, you haven't been through any fire yet." I thought I had; but I came to understand that what he meant was, I hadn't had any children yet. He told me about two of his seven children.

His son, Rex Jr., back in the 50's, was a high school All-American football player. He was being recruited heavily by college scouts from major universities. He shocked everyone by choosing to go to BYU. As a father, President Reeve was concerned that Rex would go to BYU, play football, and then eventually go on to become a professional football player. He didn't want that kind of life for his son. He sought counsel from a member of the First Presidency, who said, "Send the boy to BYU, he'll be blessed." Young Rex attended BYU and played football for one year. Then he became deathly ill and lost an incredible amount of weight. The doctors sent him home to die, saying there was nothing more they could do.

President Reeve told me this was a very dark time for him as he struggled to find the blessing that had been promised by an apostle. His son received priesthood blessings, of course, and Sister Reeve made a study of natural medicine before plying the boy with all sorts of herbal remedies. He made a full recovery, never played football again, got married in the temple and started a good-sized family, served as a mission president around the age of 30, and eventually became a professor of ancient scripture at BYU.

President Reeve's daughter, Becky, was serving a full-time mission in New Mexico when the car she was driving lost traction on a snowy road and inexplicably rolled--despite her driving carefully and at a slow speed. This resulted in her being thrown from the car. She sustained injuries to her spine that left her a C-6 quadriplegic. Her doctors told her that she would never sit up or move again. They gave her a twenty-year maximum life expectancy. President Reeve told me that he had laid his hands on his daughter's head to give her a blessing many times, with the intention of healing her outright, but the Spirit had always whispered, "Not yet." Still, all those blessings weren't for naught. After a year and a half, she had managed to move one finger on her right hand. Years later, having persevered in her efforts to regain control of her body, she was able to sit up in a wheelchair. Then she learned to type holding a pencil in her hand, using the eraser end to hit the keys. Years after that, with the help of braces, she stood up on her own two feet. And now, some 55 years after her preternatural accident, she's still going strong.

I got to know her when she came to California with her

parents to serve in the mission home. She was in a wheelchair then, always smiling, never bitter. Instead, she went on to inspire many with whom she shared her story over the years through talks, newsletters, correspondence, and books-- including "The Spirit Knows No Handicap," which has sold over 30,000 copies.

Yes, Rex C. Reeve, Sr. had been through the refiner's fire. And having passed through it, there was nothing left in his heart but love and compassion for everyone he met. He served in the First Quorum of Seventy for eleven years before receiving emeritus status. He died in 2005. The love that he freely radiated upon all who were blessed to know him will be felt and reciprocated for eternity.

Back to the Salt Mines

A Shock to the System

After my mission, trying to integrate myself into the real world again was quite a shock to the system. I found it difficult to successfully balance the spiritual with the secular. Once deprived of the discipline of the mission field, I couldn't find any worldly goal or purpose that motivated me sufficiently to discipline myself. This was perhaps the inevitable result of the disdain with which I held all secular pursuits in the wake of the spiritual upheaval that I had undergone during my conversion. This struggle was only compounded by the fact that girls were again a part of my life. I remember the first girl I kissed after my mission; I felt like I needed to schedule an appointment with the Bishop. But, as finding an eternal companion was the order of the day, I soon overcame my reticence and got back in the game.

Release the Cretin!

By way of employment, I was throwing boxes for a parcel delivery service (which shall remain nameless), working on the sorting conveyor belt. It was a great job at the time. We made $8.50 an hour; and we were members of the International Brotherhood of Teamsters. There was a certain type of box that kept coming down the belt day after day; it was roughly 3 feet long by 1 foot square, about what you would expect if it had contained a dozen long fluorescent light tubes. But the label gave us no clue, so we never knew what was in these boxes. As we handled them though, it became apparent that whatever the contents were, they had not survived the shipping process. Every time we picked one up and shook it, we heard the sound of broken glass and sand. We had never seen one come through our hub intact. We marveled at this, and wondered aloud why anyone would continue to ship these if they never arrived in one piece. We considered every possibility from gross incompetence to insurance fraud.

One day, somebody picked up one of these boxes, shook it, and it made no sound. He passed it to another worker for confirmation, who also shook it . . . nothing. Someone stopped the conveyor belt, and we passed the box from man to man so everyone could witness the miracle. When the box came to Danny, the company cretin, he shook it. And when it made no sound, he got this troubled look on his face as though he were thinking, "That ain't right." Suddenly, he hoisted the box over his head and slammed it down on the conveyor belt with all his strength. Then he picked it up and shook it again. We all heard that familiar sound of broken glass and sand. Danny seemed pleased. Someone started up the belt and we all went back to work. Everything was right again in our little world.

Shortly afterwards I quit that job when they refused to give me time off to perform with the Richmond Mormon Chorale, despite my having rehearsed with them for many months. Then, a year or so after the fact, I wrote up an account of the mystery-box event and sent it in to *Reader's Digest*. I received a terse reply that it was not the kind of story they were looking for.

Hi-Diddle-Dee-Dee, an Actor's Life for Me

I was dating a girl that I had really fallen for, named Debbie, who lived in Northern Virginia. I drove up there from Richmond as often as I could to spend time with her. One weekend she dragged me to an audition for a touring company of an LDS musical called *Saturday's Warrior*. I had heard about the show in California, and wasn't particularly interested in it. But Debbie was very excited at the possibility of becoming a member of the cast and traveling around the country for the summer. During her audition, it became apparent that she could not sing. It was grim. When she finished, the director, Michael Flynn, looked at me and said, "What about you?" "I'm just here to watch her audition." "Can you sing?" "Well . . . yeah." He convinced me to come up and give it a try. After I sang something, he asked the assistant choreographer to see if I "could move." She showed me a few simple steps, and I repeated them. Suddenly, I was cast as "Mack," the bad guy who sang two solos and danced in a couple of big production numbers. (This all didn't bode well for my relationship with Debbie.) The company toured July and August of 1979: College Park, Philadelphia, Greensboro, Cleveland, Detroit, Toronto, Norfolk, Atlanta, Rochester, Pittsburg, Columbus, Indianapolis, Nashville, Oklahoma City, Wichita, Kansas City, St. Louis, Denver, Albuquerque, El Paso, San Antonio, and Houston. The size of the house varied. We had 1600 people one night in St. Louis at the Kiel Opera House. In some cities we had two or three performances. I'll never forget any of the cast and crew;

85

we really did become like family. After each show we would sign autographs and field questions. Mostly I would get the rowdies and jack Mormons who related to my character, "Yo, Mack! You rock, buddy."

Mack Always Rings Twice

One of the leads in our production of *Saturday's Warrior* was a massive diva. We had a big production number together where he was being "roughed up" a la *Westside Story*. Each night, a member of Mack's gang would hurl him across the top of a long, high platform toward me. I would grab him, shake him around a little, and throw him back where he came from. Then, caught in between us, he would sing. One night, he came stumbling across that high platform with a little too much steam and slammed into me with such force that I was about to fall backwards into the dark off the eight-foot-high platform. Even though I had him by the shirt, I could feel myself going over the edge. Instinctively I raised my right knee to counter the momentum and caught him right between the legs. Boom! This enabled me to get my balance, but at a cost. I'll never forget the look on his face; it was, "Oh no, you didn't." Then I flung him back across the platform where he burst into song, no doubt nailing the high notes. He was a trooper, I'll give him that. The very next night--I thought he would have learned his lesson, but no, he came in just as hot as the night before--Boom! The exact same thing happened. The look on his face was twisted rage. I assume the audience thought it was all part of the show, that I was just really working him over. Afterwards, he pulled me aside and said, "If you ever do that again!" I pleaded innocence, making my case for self-preservation. He didn't buy it; but for the rest of the tour, as he came across that high platform . . . he approached me gingerly. We had an understanding.

Brigham Young University

A Bold Move

Most of the *Saturday's Warrior* cast were attending BYU, and they convinced me that Provo was the place I ought to be; so I made an application for admission. Then one day, I was waiting in the orange VW Super Beetle for a friend to come out of baggage claim at what was then National Airport. Suddenly Dallin Oaks came walking up the sidewalk. He was the president of BYU at that time (subsequently called to the Quorum of the Twelve Apostles). I recognized him from a picture in the *Ensign* magazine. Standing on the seat, I stuck my head and torso up through the open sun roof, pointed my finger at him, and shouted, "Dallin Oaks!" He spun around in my direction with a what-on-earth-is-this look on his face. Then he spotted me, and his expression softened. I added, "Wait there!" I ran over and introduced myself, telling him I was a convert and a recently returned missionary. He took a sincere interest in me despite my effrontery. I asked him if he was going to let me into BYU. He responded in his baritone voice, "How are your grades?" "They're uh . . . yeah, you know . . . they're OK." "Hmmm," he intoned; but he wrote down my name and information. That's probably how I got into BYU.

Slings and Arrows

As a college student, I attended a session of General Conference that was held in the original Tabernacle, the oval structure built by the pioneers on Temple Square in downtown Salt Lake City. The building is renowned throughout the world for its amazing acoustics. A demonstration is given daily where a pin is dropped at the pulpit and the sound reverberates throughout the hall. I was seated in the front row of the balcony only one or two sections removed from the dais and to the speaker's right. Seated next to me, slightly closer to the podium, was an elderly couple. Then it was announced that Elder Marion G. Romney would be the next speaker. As the aged apostle made his way to the podium, the hall was silent, you could have heard a pin drop. The elderly brother to my left took this occasion to say to his wife--in what I'm sure he thought was a whisper, but which in the Tabernacle sounded more like a voice one would employ at a NASCAR event-- "Oh, no, not him! He puts me to sleep every time." I turned and looked at him with an expression of disbelief on my face, thinking, "What an apostate!" I'm sure everyone in the Tabernacle heard it. Possibly people viewing at home on TV heard it. Arriving at the podium with a wry smile, Elder Romney gave his address without missing a beat.

Save that Book!

I had a friend at BYU named Hal. He too was a convert to the Church. He told me the following story. He was working in a paper recycling mill on the conveyer belt. One day a thought forcefully comes to his mind to save that book before it is destroyed. He thinks, "What book?" The thought comes, "That one at the end of the belt, hurry!" As he runs toward the shredder, he sees it. It's sky blue with a golden figure on the cover, and it's about to drop into the maw. He snatches it off the line just in time, looks at the cover and reads, "The Book of Mormon." He takes it home, reads it, prays about it, and joins the Church. Someone had obviously thrown it away. It just goes to show, you can't keep a good book down.

The Mystery of the Agency of Man

I took an aptitude test to help me choose a career path. It said I should be a philosopher. "Thanks, that helps a lot!" But I finally found a secular pursuit worth pursuing (even though it was a spiritual pursuit in secular clothing). I wanted to write a play that would engender a paradigm shift in the minds of the audience, so that they would suddenly see the truth, as I had years before. After discovering for myself that Christ's church had been restored to the earth, my only real raison d'etre was to try to help others discover that for themselves. Believing that I could accomplish that through theater, I studied playwriting.

Michael Flynn used to say that the theater was a temple, and it can be; but in my experience, it is much more likely to be a house of ill repute. Eventually I realized that people don't come to the theater to have their worldview challenged or altered; they come to have it confirmed. That's why they stone prophets, and not playwrights. Just as people don't seek out preachers who contradict their cherished beliefs and traditions, they rather hire someone to preach to them what they want to hear or what they are used to hearing. Therein lies the wisdom of allowing God to choose who will shepherd His flock here on the earth.

No, the kind of metamorphosis I was hoping to foment is only ever accomplished in one way: one person sharing the truth with another as the Holy Ghost bears witness. That's it. Everything else is window dressing. Consider the following:

"Verily I say unto you, he that is ordained of me and sent forth to preach the word of truth by the Comforter, in the Spirit of truth, doth he preach it by the Spirit of truth or some other way? And if it be by some other way it is not of God. And again, he that receiveth the word of truth, doth he receive it by the Spirit of truth or some other way? If it be some other way it is not of God. Therefore, why is it that ye cannot understand and know, that he that receiveth the word by the Spirit of truth receiveth it as it is preached by the Spirit of truth? Wherefore, he that preacheth and he that receiveth, understand one another, and both are edified and rejoice together. And that which doth not edify is not of God, and is darkness. That which is of God is light; and he that receiveth light, and continueth in God, receiveth more light; and that light groweth brighter and brighter until the perfect day." (Doctrine and Covenants 50:17-24)

The best explication of this scriptural principle that I have found comes from an early apostle of the Church, Parley P. Pratt, who wrote:

"Two balls of quicksilver [mercury] placed in contact, immediately recognize and embrace each other. Two blazes of fire, placed in near contact, will immediately spring toward each other and blend in one . . . So it is in spiritual things. There is in every man a portion of the spirit of truth; a germ of light: a spiritual test or touchstone, which, if strictly observed, studied, and followed by its possessor, will witness to him; and will, as it were, leap forward with a warm glow of joy and sympathy, to every truthful spirit with which it comes in contact: while by a shudder of disgust, it will recognize a false spirit, a lie. Call this . . . what you please; it is so, and is a law of nature.

"Herein consists the mystery of the agency of man. This is the reason why a man is under condemnation for rejecting any spiritual truth; or, for embracing any spiritual error.

"[If] A man's deeds are evil. His monitor [conscience] is unheeded; his good angel, and the good spirit within, is grieved: and, after many admonitions which are not heeded, they retire, and leave him in the dark. He loves his own. He cleaves to a lie--he rejects the truth--darkness still increases . . . On the other hand, [if] a man's deeds are good; as saith the Scriptures--'He that doeth truth cometh to the light, that his deeds may be made manifest that they are wrought in God.' He obeys this monitor within him. He welcomes to his bosom every true and holy principle within his reach--he puts it into practice, and seeks for more: his mind expands: the field of intelligence opens around, above, beneath him: wide and more widely extends the vision: the past, the present, the future, opens to his view. Earth, with its tribes; heaven, with its planets and intelligences; the heaven of heavens, with its brilliant circles of suns, and their myriads of angels and sons of God, basking in sun-beams of pure intelligence; and streams of light and love. Each adding to, and mingling in the light of the other, till the whole enlightens the vast universe, both spiritual and physical; and the vision loses itself in its very immensity, on the confines of its own infinitude."[6]

Returned Missionaries on the Lam

Matt and I were on a road trip over Christmas break: Wyoming, Utah, California. His CB handle was "Brazil Nut" because he had served a mission in Brazil. My handle was "Stewboy," after a dog that chased Parley P. Pratt on one occasion as he was escaping from jail. In Wyoming, as the new year was fast approaching, we bought some truly awesome fireworks. They were huge rockets that I'm fairly certain were illegal to sell in Utah at that time. And we also picked up some normal little bottle rockets just for grins. One night, sometime around New Year's, we ended up in Provo. We decided the time was right for the serious artillery. We were south of campus in the neighborhoods along 900 East, where I lived while attending BYU. We had two quart-size glass bottles from which we launched our missiles while hanging out of the car windows.

We put on quite a display, some two to three hundred feet over the houses in the neighborhood. It never occurred to us that someone might call the police. Ah, youth! So, you can imagine my shock--as I leaned out of the passenger side window to launch the last of the large rockets, the fuse already burning down--when I saw what looked like a police cruiser facing us from the other side of 900 East on the same residential cross street where we were stopped at a stop sign. I said to Matt, "Is that a cop?" "I think so." My right hand instinctively dropped down to hide the sizzling rocket from the officer's view. And that seemed to work, at least, until the rocket launched. It left the bottle in my hand with a swoosh, traveling slightly less than parallel to the ground and losing altitude as it made its way uninterrupted by traffic across 900 East. It then struck the concrete curb just above the pavement, turned up and 90 degrees to the left, where it did the most beautiful rooster tail you've ever seen. It arched directly over the hood of the cruiser at eye level, and then dove into the ground on the other side.

Matt and I sat frozen in our seats, observing the scene. I began to think of jail time. I don't know what Matt was thinking, probably "that was a sweet rooster tail;" he was a seriously upbeat guy. As we sat transfixed awaiting our fate, the officer, switching on his lights and siren, took a hard left turn in front of us and screamed up 900 East. Apparently, he hadn't seen the rocket come across the street; but he had gotten a real good look at it as it arched over the hood of the cruiser from his left to right. He must have thought someone had fired it directly at him, and just missed. Matt activated his turn signal, as one should in these situations, and turned left traveling slowly in the opposite direction down 900 East, watching his rearview mirror closely as we got out of Dodge.

We decided to lie low for a while. Matt pulled into the empty parking lot of an old disco dance barn called "The Star Palace," which was defunct at that time, as I recall. Once we determined that the coast was clear, we remembered that we still had the small bottle rockets. Matt, not wanting them to go to waste, took a dozen or so and, with the business end pointing up, stuffed them into his crotch for easy loading and rapid firing. But he hit a snag. As he loaded up the first round, the quart-size bottle he was holding was longer than the bottle rocket itself. So, he balanced the miniature missile in the mouth of the bottle and lit the fuse. Then, as he pointed the rocket skyward, it fell backwards into the bottle which caused the fuse to go out for lack of oxygen. Undeterred, Matt brought the bottle back inside the car and started shaking it in a downward motion to get the uncooperative bottle rocket out of there. I was watching with considerable interest at this point. As the rocket emerged, finding itself again in an oxygen rich environment, it reignited and launched down toward the firewall at Matt's feet. There it bounced around the pedals awhile before turning 180 degrees and flying directly back into Matt's lap, where it exploded.

Now, the gentle reader need not swoon, Matt went on to father five children. But that eventuality seemed very much in doubt in the moment. Matt was enveloped in smoke; and we were both stunned and temporarily deafened by the blast being at such close quarters. As our hearing returned, we noticed an odd hissing sound, and realized to our horror that the remaining bottle rockets in Matt's lap were now hot, as in lit and counting down to launch. Matt yelled, "Oh, no!" and arched his back--his efforts being thwarted by the steering wheel--as the bottle rockets began to move out in all directions. Fissst, Fissst . . . Fissst. The car was filled with smoke. I opened the passenger door and rolled out onto the asphalt as though I were bailing out of a burning plane. I ended up on my knees looking back through the open door with tears streaming down my face, laughing uncontrollably, nevertheless feeling a solemn obligation to witness the proceedings. And oddly, Matt too was laughing, which would not have been my reaction had I been the one with a crotch full of hot bottle rockets. Smoke was pouring up and over the edge of the car's roof like an upside-down waterfall. Through welling tears, I saw Matt in his awkward position just trying to hang on, waiting for it to end as the bottle rockets bounced around the interior of the car. After the last rocket was spent, Matt relaxed and I climbed back in. We checked the car for open flames; and then, being out of rockets, we called it a night.

The Road Not Taken

I met a wonderful girl named Lori. She was right out of high school and starting her first semester at BYU. She played the piano, and I liked to sing. After we had been dating for a while, we went on a hike up into the mountains to explore an old mining shaft that I was familiar with. Looking back on it now, it was incredibly dangerous. First, we had to hike up three hundred yards of rockslide at 45 degrees. Then we walked along the side of the mountain on a trail that came perilously close to sheer cliffs. Once inside, there was a wooden ladder that ascended a vertical shaft for over 100 feet. On the upper level, there was a ~2x12 plank that precariously traversed another downward shaft that was maybe 10 feet across and about 75 feet deep. On the other side of that, the tunnel became smaller and smaller until it was just a crawl space that abruptly ended. When we reached that point, I said, "Well, this is as far as we can go." At that moment, my flashlight died. I had brought some extra batteries, but batteries weren't the problem. The bulb had burned out.

We were surrounded by an absolute absence of light, a darkness that can only be experienced in the heart of a mountain. Aside from our breathing, and the rustling of our clothes, the silence was complete. The thought of having to take Lori back over that plank single file in pitch black darkness, knowing that a slow, agonizing death waited below, was sobering. And that was provided, of course, that we could even find the plank again, without tumbling into the shaft before we realized that we had reached the edge. We prayed aloud together. These were heartfelt prayers. After we prayed, as we worked our way back in the general direction of the shaft, the Spirit prompted me to sit down, with Lori behind me, and scoot forward, throwing rocks ahead of us as we went. When I threw a rock and didn't hear it hit the ground in front of me, I knew we were at the shaft. Feeling around with my hands, I found the plank. Now there was nothing else I could do to help her. At that point, we had to separately negotiate the plank. It was such a helpless feeling. But thankfully, Lori was up to the challenge. Once on the other side, we moved forward carefully. Eventually, we found the other vertical shaft with the ladder jutting up through it, and made our way back down the mountain.

We bonded over this experience, and within a short time we were engaged. But eventually, the engagement was broken off. For my part, I worried that I had fallen in love with her innocence, more than with her. At least, that was my regrettable rationale.

Lori says that she has told this story many times. The following are a few salient excerpts from her version of events (condensed and emended for continuity). She writes:

"What I remember clearly is that we came to a ladder and climbed up what felt like a four-story building. At one point, we also crawled across a seemingly bottomless pit on a board, probably 12"-18" wide. It was scary **with** the light. When we were deep inside the mountain, our flashlight suddenly went out. I thought I had known darkness before, but this was the can't-see-your-hand-in-front-of-your-face darkness, the complete-absence-of-light darkness, the mess-with-your-mind darkness that is indescribable. As reality settled in, I don't remember being terrified, or crying, or panicking. We knelt on the dusty floor of the tunnel and prayed. I didn't experience a surge of peace or confidence as we finished; but as we rose and began the slow trek out, I did not feel hopeless. The two times I was afraid were crossing the pit and descending that ladder. Feeling my way along that board, slightly disoriented in the dark, it seemed like an eternity before I reached solid ground on the other side. After those two obstacles, as we felt our way along the walls, there was a slight breeze, and I wondered if we might be nearing the entrance. Then I realized I could almost see your outline in the dark; and suddenly there were stars. It was night, stars never looked so beautiful to me."

"Lewdity," Liquor, and Laughter in Yugoslavia

In 1983, while a student at BYU, I auditioned for a musical play, *Patches of Oz,* that was set to perform in Yugoslavia. It was an original work under the direction of Dr. Harold Oaks which was based on a book entitled *The Patchwork Girl of OZ* (a sequel to *The Wonderful Wizard of OZ)*. As part of the audition, someone asked me to do a British accent, which I undertook only to have it slide into Cockney halfway through. This was followed by a German accent which morphed into French at some point. They were not impressed. As I walked out of the room the assistant director called after me, "Thanks for the tour of Europe." And yet for some reason, they cast me as the "Woosie." I had a large wooden block head and a square body that rolled around on caster wheels, and I spoke with a British accent. It seems I was intended to be "the living embodiment of a cubist painting."

Our main performance was scheduled in Shebenik, Yugoslavia. It was a live stage show that was to be broadcast nationwide on Yugoslavian Television as part of *The International Festival of the Child.* Now normally, when a performance group goes out of BYU they have a grueling schedule, something like 14 shows in 10 days, and they come home exhausted. We were going to be in Europe for two weeks, during which time we had a grand total of two performances. This remarkably relaxed schedule was the result of the group having received a large discount on airfare contingent upon our staying no less than two weeks in Europe. And the Yugoslavian Government had agreed to pick up the tab for our room and board for the ten days or so that we planned to kill in Shebenik, which was on the Adriatic coast. So, aside from a couple of rehearsals and the televised performance, we spent most of our time hitting the beaches and lounging around the hotel.

There was one girl in the cast (thankfully I don't recall her name) who was just drop dead gorgeous, way too sexy for her own good. One day she took to the beach to layout and get some sun, wearing a very revealing bikini. How revealing was it? Well, there was the bare minimum of "coverage" in square inches; but what really made it special was the fact that she had crocheted it herself; and it looked like she had used a crochet hook the diameter of a jumbo pencil. I got a good look at her handiwork as she walked by; it was a masterpiece of immodesty.

In her defense though, we had somehow been housed in a resort hotel that was situated on a topless beach, which I'm sure came as a shock to Dr. Oaks. So, when he came strolling down the walkway to the sand fully clothed and spotted one of his girls, for all intents and purposes, lying naked on the beach, he was apoplectic. The sound that came out of the man traveled up and down the beach for a hundred yards in either direction as he bellowed, "Get into the hotel, and put on some clothes!" She jumped up and scurried off toward her room.

Thinking about it now, I'm reminded of a few lines from a poem I wrote years ago, which is likely lost to arts and letters forever, and probably for the best, as it fails to set the bar very high.

> she feels light sight of eyes which hesitate
> then linger longer than too late
> embarrassed I equivocate
> if you'll excuse my rudeness
> I'll overlook your nudeness

One evening we met a middle-aged Russian man who was vacationing there. He spoke no English, but I discerned that he was a coal miner when he picked up a black rock and pointed to it. He soon realized that we were Americans, took out his wallet, gave some denari (Yugoslavian currency) to his friend, and uttered one of only two Russian words that I knew at the time, "vodka." In an effort to shut down his generous offer before it got out of hand, I broke out my other Russian word, "nyet," put the two together and said, "Nyet vodka!" At this he seemed even more enthused, and encouraged his friend to hurry. I now know that "Nyet vodki!" in Russian means, "Hey, there's no vodka!" We somehow managed to avoid an international incident by escaping before the vodka arrived.

Our rehearsals for the televised performance in Shebenik had gone smoothly; but the night of the show the entire backstage area was laced with 1-inch thick lighting and camera cables. As I went to make my entrance, my little caster wheels were out of their depth. So, I picked up my seat, leaped onto the stage, and threw the seat down like a skateboard in midair. I landed it, but rolled almost the entire length of the stage before getting it under control. It was quite the entrance. I'm sure I got the cameraman's attention.

After our performance, the mayor of Shebenik joined us for a farewell dinner. We were seated on both sides of a long table with the mayor and Dr. Oaks at the head. There was a girl in the cast who looked a lot like Marilyn Monroe. As far as the mayor was concerned, she **was** Marilyn Monroe. He openly invited her to return to Shebenik and spend some time with him at his dacha by the sea. She just blushed. We were having a very good time. There were a lot of smiles and laughter all around. I was in rare form. At one point, flipping a butter knife over in my hand and grabbing it by the blade, I vigorously thumped a bowl of steamed scampi several times in quick succession. With everyone looking at me as though I had lost my mind, I said, "I thought I saw one move." The table erupted with laughter (you had to be there). Dr. Oaks leaned over toward the Mayor, and said, "All this, and without alcohol."

Virgin River Canyon

I have driven through the Virgin River Canyon, south of St. George, Utah, many times. It's almost always a hair-raising experience; but I only recall one time when I thought I might die. I was in St. George producing a performance of *My Turn on Earth*, another LDS musical. I was also playing one of the two male leads. And for some reason that escapes me, I was being driven through the canyon by a Relief Society President in a Cadillac. I gained a new appreciation for the term "white-knuckle," as the speedometer hovered around 90 mph.

We stopped at a little convenience store. I had a few-days stubble, and I was wearing a blue, felt cowboy hat. The woman behind the counter took an inordinate interest in me as soon as I walked in. She followed my every move while I wandered around the store, as though she suspected I might steal something. I thought, "Wow, do I look that rough?" When I came up to check out, she looked me over and said, "Are you, or are you not, Peter Fonda?" And I thought, "Yeah, I can pull this off." Just then I happened to glance at the wall behind her. There were two autographed pictures, one of Henry and one of Jane. I said, "No. No, I'm not." I don't look anything like Peter Fonda; she was just desperate to get that third autograph.

Personal Fouls

After a few years in the theater department at BYU, I had a play produced as part of the main season on campus. It was mounted in the Margetts Arena Theater, less than 100 seats, three-quarter round. It was a full-length comedy, directed by Barta Heiner, called *Personal Fouls*. A friend of mine, Nyle Smith, came up with the title. Nobody liked the titles I put forward. My two favorites were *The Timely Death of Bubba Lee* and *Bubba Goes Greyhound*. My mother, brother and sister drove all the way out from Virginia to see it. It was funny. I used to sit up in the lighting rack and watch the audience doubling over with laughter. Admittedly, a lot of that had to do with the actors--who were phenomenally talented-- and Barta's remarkable gift for stage direction. After one performance, an elderly gentleman stood up in the theater and asked aloud, "Who wrote this? Where is the author?" I came down and shook his hand. He told me he was a retired theater critic from the Salt Lake Tribune. He spoke of the play in glowing terms, and added, "My wife was laughing so hard, she had to leave the theater; she was afraid she might throw up." It doesn't get much better than that. I figure roughly 1000 people saw it.

One of my favorite scenes involves an uptight MBA/ JD student, Doug, his girlfriend, Betsy, and Betsy's brother, Bubba, who is a deranged paraplegic going through the denial phase. Doug and Bubba are roommates in a basement apartment. Earlier Bubba had burned some toast and couldn't get the smoke alarm to shut up from his wheelchair, so he brought it down with a polo mallet. Then, Doug is trying to justify to Betsy why he is evicting her troubled brother.

Doug: "When I got home, I heard the smoke alarm wailing all the way from the street. I ran down the driveway and turned the corner not to see the burnt remains of the basement, no. Instead, I see your brother grilling the smoke alarm on the hibachi. He was jeering at it and poking it with a stick." Betsy: "I know he's a little off-the-wall; that's half of his charm." Doug: "No, we're not talking charm here, Betsy. He made it scream in its own smoke."

Washington, DC

DC Haiku

Growing older now
non-rush hour underground
where is the metro?

Scion of Zion

My roommate in DC was David Cannon. He was a direct
descendent of George Q. Cannon, an apostle, who is regarded
by some as a power-behind-the-throne figure in the early
Mormon church. (He led the effort in Congress to achieve
statehood for what was then the proposed state of Deseret,
a little larger than Texas, which Congress pared down to
what we know today as Utah.) Dave was, without doubt,
the most accomplished individual I had ever met. He spoke
German, having served a mission in Switzerland. He had a
J.D. from The J. Reuben Clark Law School at BYU, and a
Masters of Public Administration from the Kennedy School
of Government at Harvard University. He had clerked for
a federal judge and served as an assistant to the head of the
Federal Communications Commission. And, when I met
him, he was working in the Reagan White House as a Senior
Domestic Policy Analyst. All this, and he was in his early 30s.

Still, he wasn't all work and no play; he had a mischievous
side. Early one Sunday morning some idiot pulled up in front
of our apartment building in Crystal City and started blowing

his horn. This went on for several minutes unabated. Without either of us saying a word, we both ended up standing in front of the open refrigerator studying our options. We were drawn to the eggs. Looking out the open window from the twelfth floor, we saw the offending vehicle directly below, the driver still flailing at the horn. I managed to tag the right rear quarter panel with my egg, but Dave's exploded in the middle of the rear window. The horn went silent. Quickly shutting our window, we then took pride in our community service.

We became good friends; and a few years after we met, I worked for him as his office manager. He had put together an impressive team, including former heads of state, in an effort to establish an autonomous "Superzone" in a third world country that would offer modern infrastructure, a ready workforce, and a business environment free of corruption. It was a noble effort that failed to come to fruition.

Yeltsin on the Tank

One of the Vice Presidents of Dave's company was a very diplomatic Russian gentleman who was a recent convert to the Church. He told me that he had participated in Boris Yeltsin's government, where he worked as the assistant to one of Yeltsin's ministers. When he mentioned the fact that he had been present in the Russian White House (where their Duma meets) during the coup attempt against Gorbachev, I was fascinated. He told me that he was there when Yeltsin and some of his colleagues took refuge in the basement of the White House as Soviet tanks surrounded the building. Most of them were issued side arms, and they fully expected to be killed at any moment. Wide-eyed, I said, "So you were there when Yeltsin stood on the tank and read his declaration?" He responded in his Russian accent, "Sean, Yeltsin cowered in the basement with the rest of us. He did not stand on the tank, until your President Bush [senior] called him on the phone, and told him that your CIA had intercepted communication from coup leaders [sic] to tank commanders [sic] in the field, ordering them to fire, and they had refused . . . then, Yeltsin went and stood on the tank." He went on to explain that the CIA had been very upset with President Bush for making that call, because it revealed to the Soviets that we had the capability of deciphering their communications on the battlefield--something they did not know. I have watched two or three documentaries on the events surrounding the collapse of the Soviet Union, and not one of them mentioned that phone call.

You Said You Was High Class

Nearly every Sunday Dave and I would go "ward hopping," i.e., visiting as many singles wards as possible in the area. It wasn't a function of religious zeal, we just wanted to meet as many girls as possible. There was one girl that we were both interested in, named Mary. Dave got to her first and asked her out, but then he couldn't make the date; so he asked me to fill in for him. He said he had two tickets for the National Symphony Orchestra in the Presidential Box at the Kennedy Center that I was welcome to use. How could I not go?

It was an evening of Prokofiev and Shostakovich, under

the baton of Rostropovich. The Prokofiev selections all came from the latter Stalin years, when the composer was "encouraged" to limit himself to more conventional jingoistic themes. But, notwithstanding those constraints, the music was amazing.

So, we were feeling pretty swell, sitting behind the Presidential Seal. Although, during intermission--judging from the expressions on their faces--that didn't stop the social climbers around us from wondering, "Who let the riffraff in?" And, rightly so, I suppose. At one point, I leaned over and said to my date, whose father was a music teacher, "You know, I think Prokofiev is my favorite of the Russian composers." She scrunched up her face and said, "You've heard of these guys?"

Golf on the Sabbath

There's a joke that makes the rounds in the LDS church. A Mormon bishop is playing golf on Sunday as the Lord and Saint Peter watch from above. Saint Peter says, "What are we going to do about this?" The Lord says, "Relax, I'll take care of it." The Bishop tees it up on a short par-three and slaps it in the hole for an ace. Saint Peter says, "I thought you were going to handle it." The Lord says, "I did. Who can he tell?"

I have played golf on Sunday twice, that I recall, since becoming a member of the Church. Both times were at the Reston, Virginia municipal course, where I usually carried my bag for the exercise. The first time, as I teed it up on number one, the wind was blowing, but it was nothing to worry about. By the time I had finished the third hole, the wind gusts were approaching 60 miles an hour. It was all I could do to make my way back to the clubhouse, leaning at forty-five degrees into a howling wind that was starting to pick up debris. The second time, as I teed it up on number one, there were a few clouds in the sky, but it was nothing to worry about. After my tee shot on the fourth hole, the rain started coming down in sheets. I took refuge in the woods. Then some of the most intense lightning and thunder I've ever witnessed joined in. I found myself sitting on a fallen tree trunk, trying to keep my feet off the rain-soaked ground so I wouldn't be electrocuted if there were a lightning strike nearby.

The Judge

While living in a small apartment in Rosslyn, Virginia, not far from the Potomac, there was a neighbor across the hall who was in the habit of leaving his door ajar with the chain on. He smoked a pipe constantly, and the smell of it permeated the hallway every day. One evening, I took a Book of Mormon and wrote on the inside cover, "I know this book is true. Consider the possibilities." Then I pushed the book through the crack in the door. The next morning, as I walked past his apartment, the door was shut. Soon after that, though, we did get acquainted. He was a retired utilities judge, getting up in years. When we talked about the Church, he told me he was "an old reprobate," and that I was just wasting my time. Still, he seemed awfully lonely in there, so I dropped in on him from time to time.

One weekend he extended an invitation to have dinner with him at the extremely exclusive Cosmo Club in downtown DC, where he was a member. Joining us was the owner of the building in which we lived. It seems the judge had set me up for a sales pitch to convert my apartment to a condo. I told the owner that my only reservation was the building's proximity to the end of the runway at National Airport. To drive home that point, I stole a few lines from a stand-up comedian and said, "Yeah, it's pretty bad. Those planes start taking off early, and they just barely clear the roof of the building. One morning, in the apartment, I got up to go to the kitchen and a flight attendant told me to sit down and buckle my seatbelt." The judge laughed, but the building owner still had the bit between his teeth. I suddenly remembered reading somewhere that the rubber left behind by tires touching down on runways was scraped up and recycled. I told him I would consider going condo, if he could guarantee me the rubber recovery concession from the roof. He gave it a rest after that.

The judge died a few months later. He left me a box of assorted nuts and bolts in his will. I think I've still got some of that stuff in the garage. When his daughter was asked for the required information to do his temple work, she gladly supplied it; but somehow it got lost. The daughter sent it again. Through a series of unlikely events, the information was stolen. The daughter supplied the necessary information a third time; and finally, I made it to the temple to have his work done.

Here, There, and Back Again

Fools Rush In

Having failed to find my eternal companion in several target rich environments, eventually, I got married just to get married. The only good thing to come out of it was the birth of my daughter. But even that joy was turned into a continuous round of unimaginable emotional pain when our relationship was systematically dismantled by divorce. It was a lose-lose situation. During those days, I would break down and sob like a child every time someone mentioned my daughter's name. Sometimes, just the thought of her would reduce me to tears, no matter where I was or what I was doing. This went on for years.

I remember one day, I was standing in line to check-out of a grocery store with my daughter in my arms. She was about 3 years old. Out of the blue, she looked up at me and said, "I love you, Daddy." "Ah, I love you too sweetheart." Just then the woman ahead of us in line turned around. She was in her 50's with an extremely haggard face. Looking me in the eye, she said bitterly, "Enjoy it while you can. When they turn thirteen, you're nobody." At the time, I thought, "Yikes!" Looking back now, she made a valid point.

The Kid

I moved to Arizona and took a job fixing fire doors in the desert with Adam, a good friend from my BYU days. This was my version of joining the Foreign Legion. One day, while rolling down the freeway in Arizona, heading to Yuma for a repair, I stopped to give a ride to a young man with a guitar who was hitchhiking. He was maybe 18 years old, slight of frame with a short, patchy, reddish beard--wandering around the country with no money and no plan. He smelled putrid. I had to roll down both windows. I asked him about the guitar. He said he didn't know how to play it; he just carried it around. A scripture came to mind, "Inasmuch as ye have done it unto one of the least of these my brethren, ye have done it unto me."[7] And I thought, "Well, here he is, the least of these, my brethren." After a while I pulled off the freeway into a small town, bought him some clean clothes and toiletry items, and then rented a motel room for the night. I gave him some cash. He looked at me sideways and said, "Are you gonna be here in the room tonight?" "No, man. I have to be in Yuma in a couple of hours. This is all yours." He seemed pleased and a bit more relaxed after that. I told him all he had to do was check out by eleven the next day. Pointing out the phone in the room, I suggested that he call his parents, saying they were no doubt worried about him. He thanked me; and I got back on the road.

Books of Mormon on a Train

After drumming myself out of the Foreign Legion, I moved back to Richmond. At some point, I took a trip on Amtrak across the country to Seattle, down the west coast and home again. I packed six or seven Books of Mormon to hand out along the way. It was amazing to see how my prayer, that I would be lead to those who would be receptive, was answered. I ran out of Books of Mormon before the trip was over. I remember a few of those who received a book along with my testimony of the restored gospel.

I talked for a couple of hours with one very pleasant middle-aged woman. She gladly accepted the Book of Mormon and said, "Oh, this is wonderful. I have neighbors who are Mormon. Now we'll have something to talk about."

A few hours out from Chicago, I met a young man from Italy who was a furniture maker. His English was pretty good, and we talked for quite a while about the Church before he accepted a Book of Mormon. After a brief layover in Chicago, as I returned to the station, I saw him sitting on the wooden benches there reading the Book of Mormon as he waited for his connecting train.

I spotted a very attractive girl in her early 20's sitting alone. The Spirit was nudging me in her direction; but I thought she was too good-looking, and would probably think I was hitting on her. Still, I asked if I could sit down next to her, and she said yes. An hour and a half later, she had a Book of Mormon and I was sharing my testimony, when an elderly black man in the seat behind us said aloud, "Amen!" I'm not sure who I was talking to.

On the last leg of the journey, I was out of books and sitting alone at the front of the coach next to the lavatory, when a sophisticated looking gentleman asked if he could sit down next to me and wait until the lavatory was unoccupied. Over an hour later, as we arrived in Richmond (he never did make it to the lavatory), we were still talking about the LDS church, as well as his experiences as an African American in his church. He gave me his phone number; he was a medical doctor. I palmed his information off on a distinguished black brother who was on the High Council in Richmond. I'm not sure how that panned out.

If you don't have a copy of the Book of Mormon, you really should get one. As ancient Scripture goes, it is unique. Although the record begins in Jerusalem around 600 BC, it predominately covers God's dealings with a branch of the house of Israel that flourished in ancient America for roughly a thousand years. The Book of Mormon is priceless because it was not only written by prophets as they were inspired by the Holy Ghost, it was also translated into English by a prophet who was inspired by the Holy Ghost. Doctrinally speaking, it is pure: no linguists, no scholars, no conflicting translations. As such, it helps one interpret those passages of the Bible that have come down to us in a less-than-pristine form. The current cover of the Book of Mormon states that it is, "Another Testament of Jesus Christ," the Bible being the first. But it also serves another vital purpose. As an inexplicable artifact--the veracity of which may only be ascertained through prayer--it is intended to challenge us to ask God.

While there is plenty of evidence to support its authenticity, I am convinced that God will never allow the Book of Mormon to be irrefutably proven, archeologically, genetically, linguistically, or anthropologically until all of His children who are capable of obtaining a testimony of its truthfulness through prayer have done so. The discovery that one may ask God a question and receive an answer is arguably of equal worth to the scriptural content of the book.

An Honorary Chair

On that same train trip, my itinerary included a couple of nights in Seattle. While walking around the city on my first evening there, I noticed the many young people milling around in the streets. They seemed lost to me, with no direction in life. Two of them, a little older than the norm, were sitting in lounge chairs on the sidewalk with a sign between them that read, "The Advice People -- Advice 25 cents." They took my quarter and gave me some advice. Then we talked awhile. There was nothing memorable about it for me. The next night I ventured out again and happened to pass the same spot. The young man with whom I had spoken the night before was there holding down the fort alone. I commented on this; and he asked me if I would like to sit in. So, I pulled up a lounge chair and became an honorary member of the Advice People for the evening. During the hour or more that I was in session, business was pretty good.

Of all the young people I advised, two encounters have stuck with me. One girl, who looked to be about 17 years old, gave me a quarter and said, "I'm thinking about trying acid (taking LSD). What's your advice?" I advised against it, and told her a story about a guy I knew in high school who had dropped acid. Later that night he was arrested for standing in the middle of the road, directing traffic . . . in his underwear. But before the police arrived, some rednecks had stopped long enough to beat him up. My story seemed to make an impact. I may have done some good there. Another girl, about the same age, gave me a quarter and asked, "Is there a God?" "Yes." "And?" "Hey, one quarter, one question, one answer. What do you want from me?" Her expression made it clear that she didn't think she had gotten her money's worth. I told her how I met Mike in that jeep as evidence of God's existence. As she listened to the story, she looked at me with a contemplative stare. Then her friends dragged her off into the night.

A Hymn

I wrote a hymn, or the words to a hymn, and put them to a variation of the tune from "Simple Gifts." (What else?) I have always felt that the old Shaker tune, as employed by Arron Copland in his composition, *Appalachian Spring*, perfectly captured the ambiance of Joseph Smith's youth around the time of his experience in the Sacred Grove. But, if anyone wants to write an original tune for this, let me know.

"Joseph"

Once a prayer was uttered in a grove of trees
by a boy of fourteen on his bended knees.
He asked of the Father in the name of the Son,
out of all the churches did God have one?

Joseph had gone to seek the Lord,
having read in the Good Book that he would be heard.
His faith was unwavering, his purpose true,
as he bowed his head asking what to do.

Then the powers of darkness, his faith to destroy,
did combine to hedge the way of the boy.
And when he was all but consumed with despair,
a light descended and God was there.

Joseph had gone to seek the Lord,
having read in the Good Book that he would be heard.
He prayed, prayed to know God's will,
and the answer from Heaven is with us still.

Now the Father invited him to hear His Son,
and then Jesus told him what must soon be done.
Apostles of the Lord would be called as before,
in the Church of Jesus Christ once more.

Joseph had gone to seek the Lord,
having read in the Good Book that he would be heard.
His faith was unwavering, his purpose true,
as he bowed his head, knowing what to do.

Thus a prayer was answered in a grove of trees,
and a boy of fourteen rose up from his knees.
He'd heard from the Father and he'd heard from the Son
that the restoration had begun.

Joseph was chosen of the Lord
to publish the truth and empower the word.
He prayed, prayed to do God's will,
and the church that he founded is with us still.

Blown Away by MoTabs

I found myself attending the dedication of the Tuacahn
Amphitheatre near St. George, Utah in 1995. I was there for
a writer's conference, and didn't know that there would be a
performance by the Mormon Tabernacle Choir as part of the
opening ceremonies. My eleventh-hour attempt to get tickets
for the concert proved bootless; the event was completely sold
out. Then, as I loitered near the box office just before the
concert was to begin, a sign was placed in the window that
announced seats were available. At the last minute, they had
decided to add two rows of folding chairs in the amphitheater,
one at the very back, and one at the very front. I said, "Yes,
please." They seated me toward the center of the new front

row, where the president of the Church, Gordon B. Hinckley, along with other notables, sat facing me on the dais some 15 feet away. Immediately behind them, on abruptly ascending risers, was the Mormon Tabernacle Choir. The performance began. I felt as though they were singing for me personally in my living room. It was glorious.

A Poor Man's Symposium

Once, while living in DC, having just come out of a health food store in Alexandria, I was loading groceries into my car when a homeless man came up quietly behind me. He was standing close enough to me that when I turned around he startled me. He said he was a veteran and needed help. I gave him a ride to the shelter where he was living. Seeing the conditions there, it was troubling to consider what his life must have been like. The homeless were packed into a large open hall furnished only with row after row of cots. Most of them appeared to be alcoholics, drug addicts, con artists; and some of them were obviously mentally ill. He showed me his Navy yearbook from the Vietnam era. He was an alcoholic with missing teeth and bleeding ulcers; he was in bad shape.

We spent some time together over the course of several months. I took him to the Veteran's Hospital, the doctor just looked at me as if to say, "Why bring him in here? He's dying. We can't do anything for him." They did start to make a bridge to fill in the holes in his smile, though. One day I brought him to my apartment, gave him some clean clothes, let him take a shower and sleep in a bed for a few hours. I even bought him a bottle of wine one time. He told me about his life, how he ended up on the street after a case of domestic violence. He had gotten the worst of it, though; that's how he lost the teeth. I met the woman he had been living with. Apparently, he hit her while they were arguing, and she counterpunched with a steam iron.

He said he was from Georgia; and if he could just get down there, his people would take care of him. So, I bought him a ticket on Amtrak, put him on the train and waved goodbye. A few weeks later, I ran into him on the streets of DC. This was October. I asked him what he was doing in Washington; he was supposed to be in Georgia. He said things didn't work out for him down there. I asked him about the woman that had helped raise him, who--he had assured me--would take care of him if he could just get back home to Georgia. He said she had two grandkids living with her that were screaming and tearing around the place night and day. His nerves just couldn't take it. I asked about his best friend, who--he had assured me--had a big house all to himself where he would be welcome to stay as long as he liked, if he could just get down there. He told me that his best buddy had used a shotgun on a friend of his for messing around with his ex-wife. The house was a crime scene with yellow police tape all around it. He couldn't stay there. I told him it was getting cold in DC, surely he would be better off in Georgia, even if on the street, at least it would be warmer. He got a little perturbed with me at that point, and said that DC was his home. He had lived there for over twenty years. There was nothing left for him down in Georgia. Eventually I figured it out. He had never gone to Georgia. The whole routine was a scam. After I put him on that train, he got off at the next stop, cashed in his ticket, and started drinking.

Cal became the lead character in my next play. It was entitled, *A Poor Man's Symposium*. "Symposium," coming from the Greek, originally meant "together with wine." I suppose you would call it a tragicomedy. Creating the character of Cal didn't take much imagination. Many of the eponymous character's lines are direct quotes. The world premiere was produced in Milwaukee, and it was scheduled to go on to Chicago. The following is one of many comedic exchanges from the play.

One of the main characters, Roy (a homeless black man), is complaining about racism to a wealthy white businessman at an intersection. Roy: "I can't even cross the street without some little white man flashing in my face first." Businessman: (condescendingly) "Well, that's because if the little guy in the crosswalk signal were black, nobody would be able to see it." Roy: "They could put a brother up there with a flashing white background; that'd work, wouldn't it?" Businessman: "Well, I guess. I didn't think of that." Roy: "You're damn straight you didn't think of that! You got any spare change?"

The box office was good for our opening weekend. Two reviews came out, one was positive, one was a rave. Unfortunately, though, we had opened on September 7th, 2001, a Friday night. The following Tuesday, September 11th, the Twin Towers came down in New York. Suddenly no one was inclined to take in an evening of theater. The Milwaukee Rep closed its doors; we didn't have that option. So, we soldiered on, but the production was doomed. The only worse theatrical debacle, of which I am aware, was a production of *My Turn on Earth* that my friend Nyle Smith had put together back in 1980. They were all set to tour Washington and Oregon. While they were en route to the first venue, Mount St. Helens blew. The freeways were shut down by a thick blanket of deadly ash. The highway patrol told them to turn around and go home. So, by comparison, I don't feel too bad.

And that is how I learned the hard way that when the Spirit gives you a prompting, you don't question it, you just obey. Months before the production, when a rental contract--for what promised to be an ideal theater in Chicago--had been placed in front of me, I picked up a pen to sign it, and the Spirit spoke to me as clearly as ever in my life, "Don't sign the contract." I was incredulous. The theater was perfect, the dates were available; I would never find anything like it again. I put pen to paper, and again the Spirit said, "Do not sign the contract." I couldn't make any sense of the prompting. So, with those words echoing in my mind, I signed the contract, and the rest is history. At some point, the play may be produced again, or made into a film. If it ever happens, it will probably be under the title, *Last Train to Georgia*.

Bombs Away

I once ran sound for a regional church production of *The Music Man*, using my own computer and software that was ill-designed for that purpose. During a matinee, as "Marion the Librarian" was being performed, I prepared the next sound cue, which was "Oh Columbia, the Gem of the Ocean." But somehow, rather than bringing "Columbia" on deck, the computer prematurely took the cue. So, four minutes into an eight-minute "Marion the Librarian" dance routine, that involved two-thirds of the cast, suddenly "Oh Columbia, the Gem of the Ocean" blasted out over the loudspeakers. Everyone on stage froze in their tracks. I knew immediately there were only two options: either take the "Marion the Librarian" cue again from the beginning, which would be a total disaster, or, drag the slider bar that controlled that cue somewhere toward the middle of the recorded track, drop it, and hope for the best. I chose the latter. After no more than two or three seconds of "Oh, Columbia," as my finger lifted off the button on the mouse, "Marion the Librarian" resumed two beats prior to the point where it had been interrupted. In their minds, the dancers heard, "seven, eight," and picked up right where they had left off without missing a step. It was an act of God. Some members of the audience were unaware that anything had gone wrong. Whoever offered the opening prayer that afternoon, "Kudos."

I Dreamed a Dream

The Church has a rule that a member must wait one year after the death of a relative before temple work can be done for the deceased. Temple work consists of performing baptisms, confirmations, temple sealings (eternal marriage), etc., by proxy on behalf of the dead. Then, if the deceased individual accepts the work on the other side of the veil, it is as though they had done it themselves while they were alive on the earth. (See 1 Corinthians 15:29.)

About one year after my father died, he came to me in a dream. I have had four or five dreams in my life that were not mere dreams, but rather divine intervention. They are recognizable as such because I remember them in striking detail, whereas normally, if I remember a dream at all, the details elude me and the memory of it is ephemeral.

In my dream, I found myself in a crowded amusement park (later interpreted as the first or lowest heaven, see 1 Corinthians 15:39-42 and 2 Corinthians 12:2-4). There was a young girl standing alone, and I thought, "There's that little girl who never speaks to me." She then walked right past me without acknowledging my presence. Next, my father was walking toward me. He was wearing a uniform, as though he were in some position of authority there. I said, "What are you doing here?" "I work here." "Since when?" "Two years, now." I couldn't understand how he could have a job for two years and no one know about it. Then, leaning closer to me and drawing my attention to one of his eyes with his index finger, he showed me a contact lens that was floating on his pupil and said, "Look, I have contacts. I can see now. And I need you to help me pay for them." While still dreaming, I then woke up in a hotel room that was on the amusement park property and sat bolt upright in the bed. After that, I woke up for real, and found myself in my own bed at home.

I understood from the dream that my father could see now, from his vantage point on the other side of the veil, that the restored gospel was true, and he needed me to do his temple work for him. Over the years after my baptism, he had sat down with the missionaries two or three times, but he never did join the Church. I was so upset with him for not being baptized while he was alive, that five years after this dream, his temple work still hadn't been done. I shared this story in a Sacrament meeting one Sunday, and afterwards the bishop came up to me and said, "Five years is a long time, Sean. You should get that temple work done for your father." And so, I went to the temple where I was baptized, confirmed, washed, anointed, ordained and endowed as a proxy for my father. Because of the dream, I have no doubt that he has accepted the work on the other side.

A Well-Worn Bible

Back in Richmond, driving home from church one day, while waiting at the stoplight where Horsepen Road meets Patterson Avenue, I saw a book sprawled open on its spine in the middle of the intersection. It was obvious from the way the pages sagged to one side that they were onion skin, which usually means Scriptures. It couldn't have been there long, as it appeared that no one had run over it yet. When the opportunity presented itself, I pulled into the intersection, opened the car door and grabbed it. Someone, I surmised, had placed it on the roof of their car and forgotten about it. When the car turned at the intersection the book went straight, ending up in the road where I found it only moments later.

It was a Bible, the Old and New Testament. Upon closer inspection, it became apparent that this book represented a lifetime of biblical scholarship. The margins of nearly every page were covered with handwritten notes, insights, references and cross references. Whoever had lost this was in a panic to get it back. Embossed on the cover was the last name of the owner, and perhaps some initials. It was very close to Abernathy, but without the "h" or with a "d" in place of the "th," something like that. Anyway, the name was distinctive enough that looking it up in the phone book only produced five numbers. Around the third or fourth call I had him on the phone, an elderly gentleman who was beside himself with glee to hear that his Bible had been found. He gave me his address, and I said I would bring it over to him.

As I pulled into the complex, somewhere in the West End, a sign announced that this was a retirement community for Southern Baptists. I thought, "Oh boy, here we go." I parked and saw him coming toward me. He was quite old with a full head of white hair, a little stooped over, but smiling as we drew closer to one another. I shook his hand and gave him his Bible, complimenting him on his extensive scholarship. Opening the book, he confirmed the many years of study that had been poured into those margins, and thanked me profusely for bringing it back to him.

At some point, I said, "You know, it's no coincidence that I found your Bible." "It's not?" "No. This kind of thing happens to me all the time." I gave him one example of the many opportunities God had given me to share the restored gospel. He thought it was wonderful that I had "such a strong testimony" (his words, not mine), but he said he was a dyed-in-the-wool Southern Baptist. Then he started hesitantly fishing a five-dollar bill out of his shirt pocket. It went in and out of there a few times as we wound up the conversation before I said, "I don't want your money. What I do want is for you to come to church with me on Sunday and tell me if you don't see the Spirit of God in the eyes of the Latter-day Saints." I thought, "How can he refuse?" But he did. He said he needed to get back to his wife who was in hospice and not expected to last long. As he walked away, his head was bowed a little lower than it had been when he walked up to greet me. Or, so it seemed to me; maybe it was just the angle from which I watched him turn and go.

Why Am I Here?

One day I was having Chinese for lunch; I was well out of my normal routine and well out of my way. There was only one other person in the restaurant at the time. He was reading a Bible. I knew immediately that I had been set up again with a missionary opportunity. I asked him what he was reading. After a pause, he looked up and said, "The Bible." Then he continued to read. I asked, "What book?" Again, the taciturn reply, "Psalms." I persevered, "Which one?" He gave me a number and put his head back in his book. I pressed on, "My favorite is the 22nd Psalm because it tells of the crucifixion in considerable detail over a thousand years before it happened." He said, "Uh huh." At this point, it was obvious that the casual conversation approach wasn't going to get it done. I said, "Well, today is the day that the powers that be on the other side of the veil have decreed that you should hear about The Church of Jesus Christ of Latter-day Saints. Do you know what that is?" He looked up at me and said, "Yes, I'm a member of the Mechanicsville Ward." And I thought, "Oh. So, why am I here?"

We got acquainted after that. He was in the process of moving to North Carolina, where he was getting married and starting over. Afterwards, it occurred to me that we were probably brought together that day so that he would know what a missionary moment looked like and what to do with one when he got to his new life. I mean, when our conversation started, he didn't know that **I** was a member of the Church. And I asked him several questions, any one of which easily could have served as an entree for him to tell **me** about the restored gospel; but I got nothing. Hopefully, the next time he found himself in that situation, he had something to say.

Speaking of the 22nd Psalm

I attended synagogue with a friend one Saturday in Salt Lake City, where the rabbi was leading the reading of the Torah. This went on for quite a while. The reading was in Hebrew, so I followed along in the English translation that was provided in the program. As the 22nd Psalm was read, I noticed that the wording was significantly different from that found in the King James Bible. Where the Bible read, "They have pierced my hands and feet," the Torah read, "The lion has gnawed my hands and feet." After the reading, there was a little munch and mingle. I took the opportunity to ask the rabbi about the discrepancy. He brushed it aside, saying, "The

Christians altered the words of the 22nd Psalm, so they could claim it was about Jesus." I thought about that for a moment. Then I pulled out my smartphone and looked up the 22nd Psalm in the Dead Sea Scrolls, which were written no later than the first century by a group of Essences in the desert who had nothing to do with Christianity. The translation read, "They have pierced my hands and feet." I said, "Rabbi, a word." As I was explaining my discovery, I offered to show him the Dead Sea Scroll translation on my phone. He interrupted me, saying, "I'm sorry, I can't use any electronic device on Shabbat."

In retrospect, it is a moot point. Even if you translate the line "The lion has gnawed my hands and feet" (the lion being the well-established symbol of the tribe of Judah), the text is clearly foretelling the crucifixion, which is why Jesus quoted from it as he hung on the cross. The 22nd Psalm begins, "My God, my God, why hast thou forsaken me?" Most of the Jews who were present and heard Jesus speak those words as he was dying, knew that he was referencing the 22nd Psalm. He didn't have to quote the whole thing. They heard it echoing in their minds.

[There is more to the controversy surrounding the 22nd Psalm. I feel the need to set the record straight. The line in question above appears twice in the Dead Sea Scroll fragments; in one instance, the key word is illegible, in the other instance, we find the word "kaaru." The problem is, nobody knows what "kaaru" means. Nobody. Because it's not a Hebrew word; it doesn't mean anything. Some say it is a misspelling of "karu" which means to dig, i.e., dig a well, dig a grave, etc. (There are several other words in Hebrew that actually mean "to pierce," but none of them were employed in the passage.) Others say it is a misspelling of "kaari" (as the Hebrew word actually appears in the Masoretic text) which means "like a lion;" but, "like a lion, my hands and feet" doesn't help much either. So, all the possible ways to twist the text in an attempt to make sense of it are problematic.]

Can I Get a Witness?

At this point in my life, having not yet found my eternal companion, I looked back over my discipleship in horror. I had proven to be a far-less-than-exemplary Latter-day Saint. Over the years, the waywardness that I had eschewed so completely when I joined the Church had on occasion resurfaced. The transformation that the Holy Ghost had undertaken in my life upon my entering the strait and narrow way was proving to be a longer and more convoluted process than I had hoped, with serious setbacks and periods of very limited growth (ergo, it's better to start that process sooner rather than later). For many years, I seemed to be caught up in a whirlwind of consequences. But I survived it by following the advice that Joseph Smith gave to his cousin George, during a difficult time in his life. George A. Smith records the following: "He told me I should never get discouraged, whatever difficulties should surround me, if I was sunk in the lowest pit of Nova Scotia and all the Rocky Mountains piled on top of me, I ought not to be discouraged but hang on, exercise faith, and keep up good courage and I should come out on the top of the heap at last."[8]

Still, to my way of thinking, I had really made a hash of it. Given the spiritual experiences that accompanied my conversion, I thought I should have accomplished more in building up God's kingdom on the earth. I knew other members of the Church, who did not have such vivid spiritual experiences to share, and yet they had run circles around me in every aspect of Christian discipleship. Even though my testimony of the truthfulness of the restored gospel had never wavered, not in the least, I had somehow failed to continue as I had begun. Consequently, I was deeply concerned that Heaven, at that juncture, might consider me persona non grata. I began to pray to know that my sins had been forgiven, desiring to know as Enos knew. Enos was a contributor to the Book of Mormon who describes his prayerful struggle to know that his sins were forgiven in Enos 1:2-8.

2 And I will tell you of the wrestle which I had before God, before I received a remission of my sins.
3 Behold, I went to hunt beasts in the forests; and the words which I had often heard my father speak concerning eternal life, and the joy of the saints, sunk deep into my heart.
4 And my soul hungered; and I kneeled down before my Maker, and I cried unto him in mighty prayer and supplication for mine own soul; and all the day long did I cry unto him; yea, and when the night came I did still raise my voice high that it reached the heavens.

5 And there came a voice unto me, saying: Enos, thy sins are forgiven thee, and thou shalt be blessed.

6 And I, Enos, knew that God could not lie; wherefore, my guilt was swept away.

7 And I said: Lord, how is it done?

8 And he said unto me: Because of thy faith in Christ, whom thou hast never before heard nor seen. And many years pass away before he shall manifest himself in the flesh; wherefore, go to, thy faith hath made thee whole.

I wanted to know with that same degree of certainty that my sins were forgiven. I wanted to hear a voice or see an angel. This went on for a couple of months, during which my daily prayers included the request to know, as Enos knew, that my sins had been forgiven.

Then one Sunday, I was sitting at the back of the chapel waiting for a Sacrament meeting to start. Seated next to me was one of the young full-time missionaries, Elder Head, with whom I had served on a few member-missionary teaching visits. He suddenly leaned over and whispered, "Hey, Brother Stewart, I've got a scripture for you, one of my favorites, check it out, Doctrine and Covenants, section 62, verse 3." Opening my Scriptures, I read the following: "Nevertheless, ye are blessed, for the testimony which ye have borne is recorded in heaven for the angels to look upon; and they rejoice over you, and your sins are forgiven you." As I looked up from reading, Elder Head leaned over again and said, "Isn't that awesome?" I agreed that it was; but in my mind I was saying, "That's it? That's what I get? No voice? No angel?" As I mulled it over, the Spirit whispered to me, "What greater witness can you have than from God?" These words I immediately recognized as those the Lord had spoken to Oliver Cowdery through the Prophet Joseph in Doctrine and Covenants 6:22-24.

22 Verily, verily, I say unto you, if you desire a further witness, cast your mind upon the night that you cried unto me in your heart, that you might know concerning the truth of these things.
23 Did I not speak peace to your mind concerning the matter? What greater witness can you have than from God?
24 And now, behold, you have received a witness; for if I have told you things which no man knoweth have you not received a witness?

That was the first and only time Elder Head said he had a scripture for me; and there was no way he could have known what I had been praying about. So, with that, I was more than content, I was happy in the knowledge that my sins were blotted out, to be remembered no more.

All's Well that Ends Well

Over the many years since I found out what a Latter-day Saint was, I have: studied with the missionaries and undergone the conversion process; been through the temple ordinances for myself and for my dead ancestors; served a two-year full-time mission alongside the descendants of the pioneers; toured the country in a couple of LDS musicals (staying as a guest in the homes of Church members); matriculated at two LDS universities where I studied for a total of 5 years; attended a multiplicity of LDS singles wards and family wards scattered across the country; and held many callings along the way. I have a pretty good handle now on just who the Mormons really are. In my experience, the most Christlike people on the planet are found among them. Having been a member of The Church of Jesus Christ of Latter-day Saints for over 40 years now, I could not possibly be happier with the choice I made to be baptized. As Joseph Smith said, "Happiness is the object and design of our existence; and will be the end thereof, if we pursue the path that leads to it."[9]

A great deal of the happiness that I have thus far experienced as a member of the Church is a direct result of my finally having been sealed in the House of the Lord to my eternal companion for time and eternity. But before that could happen, I had to go halfway around the world to find her. We met in Ukraine while I was working there on a video shoot. (I spoke rudimentary Russian at the time.) My future wife, Tetiana, was one of the people I interviewed. Which means, I have an hour of video of my wife on the day we met.

Who can say that? She wasn't a member of the Church at the time; but when I told her about the restored gospel, she took to it immediately. A few months later, after studying with the sister missionaries, she was baptized. Then we were married in a civil ceremony in Kiev. After that, we had a series of honeymoons (Egypt, Carpathian Mountains, etc.) while we waited 18 months for her to get her visa to the US. Once my lovely bride was allowed into the country, we were sealed in the Washington, DC temple. Now we live in Salt Lake City and attend a Russian branch of the Church where I preside over the Sunday School, and Tetiana serves as the Relief Society President. She's a better member of the Church than I am. We speak Russian at home most of the time; and we have friends now from all over the Russian-speaking world. We are planning to serve a mission together as a couple someday. Tetiana wants to serve a temple mission in Kiev. I'm not opposed to that; though, I would prefer to knock on doors in Siberia. But the recent laws enacted by the Duma prohibiting proselytizing of any kind in Russia make that unlikely. So, we will go wherever we are called and be happy to serve in any capacity.

[Well, I suppose that this must serve as the end of the book for those who are unwilling to even entertain the notion of ever making the attempt to ask God. For those who are open to the possibility of receiving an answer to sincere prayer, please read on. In the following addendum, I will try to explain why it is in your best interest to make the attempt, drawing from the Scriptures, both modern and ancient.]

There's Good News
and There's Bad News

First the Good News

The Prophet Joseph said, "Could you gaze into heaven five minutes, you would know more than you would by reading all that ever was written on the subject."[10] He was privileged to gaze into heaven on many occasions. As a result, much that is only hinted at in the Bible is expanded upon or fully explained in the Doctrine and Covenants (in conjunction with the Book of Mormon and the Pearl of Great Price). Perhaps the best news to come out of the revelations of the restoration is that 99.9% of all the people who ever have lived, or yet will live, on the earth will dwell for eternity in a heaven of one of three differing degrees of glory--one like the sun, one like the moon, and one like the stars. (Again, I refer you to 1 Corinthians 15:39-42 and 2 Corinthians 12:2-4.) So, under the rubric of "The News," let us consider in greater detail what the restoration of the fullness of the gospel of Jesus Christ has taught us about heaven (drawing from section 76 of the Doctrine and Covenants).

They who inherit that glory like the sun embrace the fullness of the gospel when they hear it preached in the flesh, and lay claim to the cleansing power of the atonement through the sacred ordinances of baptism and the laying on of hands for the gift of the Holy Ghost by God's authorized servants; then--after they have proven themselves "valiant

in the testimony of Jesus," and have overcome the world
by faith--they are sealed by the Holy Spirit of promise and
become members of the Church of the Firstborn. Also, these
are they who died without hearing the fullness of the gospel
preached, who would have embraced it wholeheartedly if they
had heard it preached. These lay claim to the cleansing power
of the atonement through saving temple ordinances which are
performed by proxy. This is the only degree of glory where
eternal marriage exists. Here we find the Father, the Son,
and the Holy Ghost. Those who obtain this degree of glory
become one with the Father as the Father is one with the Son
(see John 17). They inherit all that the Father has.

They who inherit that glory like the moon start down
the path of meeting the requirements mentioned above, and
thus lay claim to the cleansing power of the atonement, but
they then fail to be "valiant in the testimony of Jesus," and
the light of their lamps falters for want of oil. Also included
are those who reject the fullness of the gospel when they
hear it preached in the flesh, but accept it after death, laying
claim to the cleansing power of the atonement through saving
temple ordinances which are performed by proxy. They are
the honorable men and women of the earth who were blinded
by the craftiness of men. And lastly, these are they who died
without God's law, who would **not** have embraced the gospel
wholeheartedly had they heard it preached in the flesh. In this
degree of glory, men and women remain single for eternity.
Here we find the Son and the Holy Ghost; but where the
Father dwells, these may not come, worlds without end.

They who inherit that glory like the stars (where

individual degrees of glory differ, as one star differs from another in brightness) are everyone else. They have rejected-- or have been disqualified from--the cleansing power of the atonement. They must pay the price for their sins themselves in hell to the uttermost farthing. But hell has an end (explained in greater detail below); and having there paid the price for their sins, they then emerge to dwell in the least glorious of God's many mansions. In this degree of glory men and women remain single for eternity. Here we find the Holy Ghost; but where the Father and the Son dwell, these may not come, worlds without end.

And finally, there are those who, after passing through hell, are found to be filthy still. These are cast into outer darkness with Satan and his followers, for they have become devils themselves while in the flesh, and are thus unworthy to inherit a degree of glory. Those who have lived on the earth and then go on to this condemnation are extremely few in number.

Now the Bad News

The "third heaven," that Paul speaks of in 2 Corinthians 12:2-4, is the same as the "glory of the sun" mentioned in 1 Corinthians 15:39-42. Those who fall short of this degree of glory will not live as husband and wife for eternity. They will have no spiritual posterity. The authority to bind together a man and a woman on earth so that they will be bound together in heaven is only found in The Church of Jesus Christ of Latter-day Saints. I am unaware of any other Christian church that even pretends to have it. So, if being sterile and living a solitary existence for eternity, without being bound to the love of your life as husband and wife-- albeit in a "perfect" world free of scarcity, disease, and death, but one also devoid of children--is your idea of heaven, carry on. If you wish to live for eternity in such a world, where you will never again hear the laughter of a child, then you're all set.

If, however, being married to the love of your life and creating and nurturing new human life with that person is your very definition of heaven, then you need to go to the House of the Lord and be bound together as husband and wife for eternity by the authority of God's holy priesthood and the keys of the kingdom that have been restored in the latter days. I can't overstress the urgency of the matter; we know from the Bible and from modern revelation that this authority to bind must be exercised before the resurrection. Men and women cannot be bound together as husband and wife for eternity after the resurrection; it must happen before the resurrection! (To understand why this is so, prayerfully ponder again 1 Corinthians 15:39-40.)

This principle is found in the Bible in Matthew 22:23-30. Jesus is being questioned hypothetically by the Sadducees about seven brothers who were all married in succession (as one died after another) to the same woman while in the world. Whose wife would she then be in the resurrection? This was an attempt by the Sadducees (who did not believe in the resurrection) to throw the doctrine of their rivals, the Pharisees (who did believe in the resurrection), in Christ's face, as He too taught the resurrection. The underlying assumption in their taunt was that, if there was to be a resurrection, men and women would live as husband and wife afterwards, which assumption Christ did not refute. In verses 29-30 Jesus answered, "Ye do err, not knowing the scriptures, nor the power of God. For in the resurrection they neither marry, nor are given in marriage, but are as the angels of God in heaven." In the scenario presented to Christ, none of the marriages were eternal marriages performed by God's binding authority. The Jews at that time did not have that authority, as it had been taken from them with the departure of Elijah. This is why Elijah (Elias in Greek) was present on the Mount of Transfiguration, to restore the authority to "bind on earth so that it be bound in heaven," the very authority that Jesus had promised Peter only a few days before that supernal event. After this authority was again removed from the earth by the great apostasy and the death of the original apostles, Peter, and subsequently Elijah (see Malachi 4:5-6), then appeared to Joseph Smith and Oliver Cowdery and restored it piecemeal to them, which is how we have it today (explained in greater detail below). Any marriage performed without said authority ends at death, leaving the former husband and wife single for eternity. Jesus easily could have said--but did NOT say--that no one would live as husband and wife in holy matrimony after the resurrection. He said that **no one would get married** after the resurrection ("they neither marry [men], nor are given in marriage [women]"). Explaining said authority, to bind a man and a woman together as husband and wife on earth, so that they would be bound as husband and wife in heaven, to the Sadducees, who taught that the

140

resurrection was nonsense, would have been casting pearls before swine.

The Lord explained it thus by revelation to Joseph Smith in Doctrine and Covenants 132:15-16: "Therefore, if a man marry him a wife in the world, and he marry her not by me nor by my word, and he covenant with her so long as he is in the world and she with him, their covenant and marriage are not of force when they are dead, and when they are out of the world; therefore, they are not bound by any law when they are out of the world. Therefore, when they are out of the world they neither marry nor are given in marriage; but are appointed angels in heaven, which angels are ministering servants, to minister for those who are worthy of a far more, and an exceeding, and an eternal weight of glory." The same revelation goes on to explain that if anyone should usurp this authority to officiate a marriage for this life and the next, it is void, because it wasn't done by one holding the keys of the kingdom, which is the authority of the holy priesthood to "bind on earth, that it be bound in heaven."

The News Digest

So, with very few exceptions, none of God's children who experience mortality are going to spend eternity racked by inextinguishable torment. Think about it! What loving Father could do that to his child simply because he or she fell short of the high standards embraced by their more enlightened brothers and sisters? The Lord explained it thus in Doctrine and Covenants 19:6-10, "Nevertheless, it is not written that there shall be no end to this torment, but it is written *endless torment* . . . I am endless, and the punishment which is given from my hand is endless punishment, for Endless is my name." No, the widely accepted concept of eternal torment will only be experienced in outer darkness by Lucifer and those fallen spirits who followed him in open rebellion against God before the earth was formed, along with a very few who proved themselves to be wholly evil in mortality. Therefore, while the torment of hell will have an end for practically all of God's children who are consigned to it, the consequences of rejecting the fullness of the gospel of Jesus Christ will last for eternity. Those who fall short of that glory like the sun (which most glorious kingdom is our home, whence we all come), though they may qualify to dwell in a lesser kingdom of glory, their ability to progress in eternity will be severely curtailed: they will never have an increase, they will never have any spiritual offspring, they will never be allowed to return home to that kingdom where God the Father dwells.

Out of All the Churches, Does God Have One?

Why Was the Restoration Necessary?

There are over 30,000 distinct Christian churches (depending on how you count them and who you ask).[11] These different sects came into existence predominately because one group after another over 2000 years disagreed among themselves concerning the doctrine of Christ and split into two groups, and so on. This occurred despite all of them being dependent upon roughly the same Bible for a knowledge of said doctrine ("roughly" being the operative word, as there are nearly a thousand translations of the Bible in English alone). Some contend that since all these differing Christian churches teach that Jesus is the Christ (more or less), the rest of their conflicting doctrines are of no consequence, and they have all the authority they need. Contrast that attitude to that found in Matthew 7:13-14, "Enter ye in at the strait gate: for wide is the gate, and broad is the way, that leadeth to destruction, and many there be which go in thereat: Because strait is the gate, and narrow is the way, which leadeth unto life, and few there be that find it." Do you think that the "few there be that find it" is in reference to the approximately 2.5 billion Christians on the planet? And again, in Ephesians 4:4-5, "There is one body, and one Spirit, even as ye are called in one hope of your calling; One Lord, one faith, one baptism."

The original apostles obviously thought that it was

important to keep the doctrine of Christ intact, as it had been delivered to them. That's why their writings contain warnings concerning teachers of false doctrines who had already arisen, and would yet arise, from within the church. They also tell of the fight they put up to keep the doctrine from becoming corrupted--a fight that they eventually lost, which ushered in the great apostasy.

From Paul, we read in Acts 20:29-30, "For I know this, that after my departing shall grievous wolves enter in among you, not sparing the flock. Also of your own selves shall men arise, speaking perverse things, to draw away disciples after them." And in 2 Thessalonians 2:3, "Let no man deceive you by any means: for that day [the second coming of Christ] shall not come, except there come a falling away first." And in Galatians 1:6-7, "I marvel that ye are so soon removed from him that called you into the grace of Christ unto another gospel: Which is not another; but there be some that trouble you, and would pervert the gospel of Christ." And again in 2 Timothy 4:2-4, "Preach the word . . . exhort with all longsuffering and doctrine. For the time will come when they will not endure sound doctrine; but after their own lusts shall heap to themselves teachers, having itching ears; And they shall turn away their ears from the truth, and shall be turned unto fables."

From Peter, we read in 2 Peter 2:1-2, "But there were false prophets also among the people, even as there shall be false teachers among you, who privily shall bring in damnable heresies, even denying the Lord that bought them, and bring upon themselves swift destruction. And many shall follow their pernicious ways; by reason of whom the way of truth shall be evil spoken of."

From Jude, we read in Jude 1:3-4, "Beloved . . . it was needful for me to write unto you, and exhort you that ye should earnestly contend for the faith which was once delivered unto the saints. For there are certain men crept in unawares . . ."

From John, we read in 1 John 2:18-19, "Little children, it is the last time: and as ye have heard that antichrist shall come, even now are there many antichrists; whereby we know that it is the last time. They went out from us, but they were not of us; for if they had been of us, they would no doubt have continued with us." And in 3 John 1:9-10, "I wrote unto the church: but Diotrephes, who loveth to have the preeminence among men, receiveth us not. Wherefore, if I come, I will remember his deeds which he doeth, prating against us with malicious words: and not content therewith, neither doth he himself receive the brethren, and forbiddeth them that would, and casteth them out of the church." And finally, in the Book of Revelation, when John writes to the seven churches in Asia circa 90 AD, nearly all are beset by apostasy.

If the true gospel, as taught by Christ's chosen apostles, was dismissed so easily by those who called themselves followers of Christ, and this done while the original apostles were yet alive, what chance did it have after they were dead?

Because the true doctrine of Christ was corrupted, it had to be restored. The reformers recognized the problem, but, living centuries before the restoration, they had to content themselves with reformation. Nonetheless, their invaluable contributions laid the groundwork for others--chief among them, Joseph Smith--to eventually restore the fullness of the gospel of Jesus Christ. And just as importantly, restore it in conjunction with the other component of God's plan for His children which was lost in the great apostasy, namely, the authority to act in God's name on the earth. Consider again Christ's words to Peter in Matthew 16:19: "And I will give unto thee the keys of the kingdom of heaven: and whatsoever thou shalt bind on earth shall be bound in heaven: and whatsoever thou shalt loose on earth shall be loosed in heaven." (This refers to all the ordinances of the gospel: baptism, the laying on of hands, eternal marriage, etc.)

The Church of Jesus Christ of Latter-day Saints claims to have received the authority of the holy Melchisedek priesthood (see Hebrews 5:5-10) when Peter, James and John appeared to Joseph Smith and Oliver Cowdery in May of 1829 (near the border between New York and Pennsylvania, along the banks of the Susquehanna River), laid their hands upon their heads and ordained them.[12] Then, over the course of several years, additional priesthood keys (including the authority to "bind on earth that it be bound in heaven" mentioned above) were received from other heavenly messengers, Elijah and others, until the restoration of the keys of the kingdom of heaven was complete.[13] Do you think it would be in your best interest to find out for yourself if that claim is true? If so, you will need to make the attempt. It is the only way you are ever going to know.

God has always worked through His authorized servants,

whom He has chosen, not through would-be servants, no matter how well-meaning, who have chosen Him. Consider Christ's words to His apostles in John 15:16: "Ye have not chosen me, but I have chosen you, and ordained you, that ye should go and bring forth fruit, and that your fruit should remain."

The process of becoming an apostle is spelled out unmistakably in the New Testament, and that process is not simply standing up one day and announcing, "I am now an apostle." As we read in Acts 1:16-26, when the original apostles had to fill a vacancy in the Quorum of the Twelve, they selected from among those who had been with them from the beginning of Christ's ministry, and then prayed that God would reveal to them whom He had chosen. They did not ask, "OK, who's feeling it?" Neither did they announce that there was no need to call another apostle, because anyone could be an apostle whenever the mood struck them.

The founder of the first Baptist church in America, Roger Williams, after a short while, left the church he had founded to become a "seeker." As such, his writings indicate, he believed that no properly organized church existed in his day, that unless Christ Himself sent apostles to organize His church with authority, there was nothing to be done.[14] Enter the restoration, problem solved. I'm certain that he has accepted the restored gospel on the other side of the veil, as well as the saving ordinances that have been performed by proxy on his behalf in the House of the Lord.

A Bible, We Have Got a Bible

Many contend that the Bible is complete, that the canon of Scripture is closed. They claim there is no other Scripture than that contained in the Bible, as we know it, based on John's words in Revelation 22:18-19, "If any man shall add unto these things, God shall add unto him the plagues that are written in this book: And if any man shall take away from the words of the book of this prophecy, God shall take away his part out of the book of life, and out of the holy city, and from the things which are written in this book." The problem with this line of logic is that when John wrote the Book of Revelation, the New Testament had not yet been compiled, much less compiled in the order that we have it today, with the Book of Revelation coming at the end. The apostle John obviously penned that warning in reference to the words of the book he had just finished writing, or as he puts it, "the words of the book of **this prophecy**." (Moses included the same injunction as he was finishing the Torah; he wrote in Deuteronomy 4:2, "Ye shall not add unto the word which I command you, neither shall ye diminish ought from it, that ye may keep the commandments of the Lord your God which I command you." Surely, we are not going to toss out everything after Deuteronomy.) But then, concerning the Book of Mormon, the point is moot. The first third of the Book of Mormon took place and was written down long before John was born. And the primary source material for all but a few pages of the rest of it also predates the Book of Revelation.

Furthermore, the authors of the Old and New Testament make reference to many books of Scripture that we don't have today, which have been lost. In the Old Testament, we read about the existence of: The Book of Jasher (Joshua 10:13), the books of Samuel the Seer, Gad the Seer, and Nathan the Prophet (1 Chronicles 29:29), the visions of Iddo the Seer, and the prophecy of Ahijah the Shilonite (2 Chronicles 9:29), and so on. In the New Testament, we read about the existence of an epistle from Paul to the Corinthians that predates 1 Corinthians (1 Corinthians 5:9), and an epistle from Paul to the church at Laodicea (Colossians 4:16). Do you really think that Paul, in his entire ministry, only wrote thirteen (fourteen if you count Hebrews) letters to the far-flung Christian churches that he had built up? That Peter only wrote two letters? That John, who was apparently alive 60 years after Christ's earthly ministry, only wrote three letters to the faithful in all that time? All we have from Jude is one letter, in which he quotes from the prophecy of Enoch; is there a Book of Enoch in your Bible? (And then, of course, there are the scholars casting doubt on who actually wrote what and when. Thankfully, that bottomless pit is filled in by modern revelation.)

Consider the last words of the Gospel of John, John 21:25: "And there are also many other things which Jesus did, the which, if they should be written every one, I suppose that even the world itself could not contain the books that should be written. Amen." And also in Acts 1:2-3, "Until the day in which he [Christ] was taken up, after that he through the Holy Ghost had given commandments unto the apostles whom he had chosen: To whom also he shewed himself alive after his passion by many infallible proofs, being seen of them forty days, and speaking of the things pertaining to the kingdom of God." What did Jesus say to the apostles pertaining to the kingdom of God for forty days? We don't know! Either no one wrote it down, or it was written down and lost.

Maybe He explained baptism for the dead. Based on the four Gospels, there is no mention of any such ordinance before Christ's death and resurrection; and yet, in 1 Corinthians 15:29, Paul seems to know all about it--and assumes that the Christians at Corinth do as well--as he casually refers to it (while making his case for the resurrection) as though it were a common practice in the church. He doesn't try to explain baptism for the dead, nor does he speak of it as though he were introducing a new doctrine. It is a given that both the author and his intended audience are familiar with the practice. During those forty days, maybe Christ explained the three degrees of glory in great detail, enabling Paul to make a passing reference to that doctrine a few verses later in 1 Corinthians 15. How much doctrine do you think Jesus could deliver to his apostles over the course of 40 days? And we have no record of what He taught them, only that He did. Oh, if only He, through the Holy Ghost, were still giving revelation and commandments to His personally chosen apostles in our day!

Personal Revelation

Blessed Art Thou

My goal in writing this book was never to convince the reader, by making a theological argument, that the LDS Church is everything it claims to be. Even if I could accomplish that, it would do you little good. To take full advantage of all the blessings afforded mankind by the restored gospel of Jesus Christ, you will have to find out for yourself that it is true, by making the attempt to ask God. If you don't want to know, don't make the attempt. If the truth is too disruptive to contemplate, then carry on. God still loves you; and He has prepared a place for you--not the place you might have inherited as a joint heir with Christ in the presence of your heavenly Father, but a heavenly place nonetheless. If, on the other hand, you want to know that Jesus is the Christ, and that His chosen and authorized apostles are again found upon the earth, and not have it made known to you by man, but by your Father who is in heaven through His Holy Spirit, you will need to make the attempt.

Consider Matthew 16:15-17: [N.B. This occurred before Peter heard the voice of the Father on the mount of transfiguration declaring that Jesus was his beloved Son in whom he was well pleased.] "He [Jesus] saith unto them, But whom say ye that I am? And Simon Peter answered and said, Thou art the Christ, the Son of the living God. And

Jesus answered and said unto him, Blessed art thou, Simon, Bar-jona: for flesh and blood hath not revealed it unto thee, but my Father which is in heaven. And I say also unto thee, That thou art Peter [in Greek, petros, meaning a small stone], and upon this rock [in Greek, petra, meaning bedrock] I will build my church; and the gates of hell shall not prevail against it. And I will give unto thee the keys of the kingdom of heaven: and whatsoever thou shalt bind on earth shall be bound in heaven: and whatsoever thou shall loose on earth shall be loosed in heaven."

The common misinterpretation of this scripture is that Christ is saying that Peter is the rock on which He will build His church. Jesus was merely making a play on words between Peter's nickname (small stone or rock, which Jesus himself had given him), and the bedrock upon which His church was to be build up. He never intended to suggest that He would build His church on a small stone named Peter. Peter is not the bedrock; a certain knowledge, borne of the Holy Ghost, that Jesus is the Christ is the bedrock. We know that the Father revealed the true nature of Jesus to Peter **through the Holy Ghost** based on 1 Corinthians 12:3, "No man can say [meaning that he actually knows] that Jesus is the Lord, but by the Holy Ghost."

Therefore, the bedrock upon which Christ in this scripture said He would build His church is the bedrock of personal revelation; a personal revelation from God the Father, through the Holy Ghost, to the sincere seeker of truth, that Jesus is "the Christ, the son of the living God" (as had occurred with Peter), that the strait gate is baptism

in His name and receiving the gift of the Holy Ghost
from His servants who hold the keys of the kingdom, and
that the narrow way is striving to be obedient to God's
commandments as revealed by those same servants.

This personal revelation that Peter received is available to
all God's children. You too can receive it, if you will only ask.
No one can make the attempt for you. It's all on you. Make
the attempt, don't make the attempt; then live eternally with
the consequences. But, for those so inclined, take heart, in
addition to that found in James 1:5, God has left us another
promise in the Book of Mormon (the second scriptural
witness that Jesus is the Christ, written by his "other sheep,"
see John 10:16). In Moroni 10:4-5 we read, "And when ye
shall receive these things, I would exhort you that ye would
ask God, the Eternal Father, in the name of Christ, if these
things are not true; and if ye shall ask with a sincere heart,
with real intent, having faith in Christ, he will manifest the
truth of it unto you, by the power of the Holy Ghost. And
by the power of the Holy Ghost ye may know the truth of all
things."

Contrast that promise of personal revelation to the mental
exercise that produced the following affirmation I recently
saw proudly displayed on a billboard. Across the top it read,
"Beyond Reasonable Doubt," below that in larger letters,
"Jesus is Alive," and under that was a phone number. Imagine
if Peter had expressed such a testimony. How might that
have sounded when the Lord asked His disciples, "But whom
say ye that I am? And Simon Peter answered and said, 'I'm
convinced beyond reasonable doubt that thou art the Christ,

and I'm not discounting the notion that, as thou sayest, thou art the son of . . . of . . . uh . . . you know, God.' And Jesus answered and said unto him, 'Blessed art thou, Simon, Bar-jona: for thou hast heard the arguments, pro and con, and given it some thought.'" That's the difference between having the divinity of Jesus Christ made known to you by your Father in heaven through His Holy Spirit, and having it made known to you by man.

So, let's suppose that you really do want to know if it's true that Jesus is--as Peter boldly declared--"the Christ, the Son of the living God," and that the keys of the Kingdom of God have been entrusted to man again under the auspices of His holy priesthood, but for some reason, you are unwilling to make the attempt to ask God. What does that leave you? What's the alternative? Are you going to read every word ever written on the concept of God, and then take Emanuel Kant's *Critique of Pure Reason* as your guide to do the "a priori/a posteriori" dance, as though it were the tarantella, until you have an epiphany of logic? What a flaming waste of time! You're never going to know anything about God with certainty until God reveals it to you. And He has promised to do just that, but only if you are willing to make the attempt.

Or, let's suppose that you already know by God's Spirit that Jesus is "the Christ, the Son of the living God," but you don't know whether or not the keys of the Kingdom of God have been entrusted to man again under the auspices of His holy priesthood. What now? Are you going to blindly trust in the traditions of your fathers, as most of the Jews did in Christ's day? (Bear in mind that the Jewish tradition in Christ's day was every bit as based in revelation from God and actual events as is the modern Christian tradition today.) Are you going to put your head in the sand and hope it goes away? Or, are you going to make the attempt, exercise your faith, and ask God?

Is You Is, or Is You Ain't
a Latter-day Saint?

What Does Jesus Think about Christians?

Matthew 25:1-12

1 Then shall the kingdom of heaven be likened unto ten virgins, which took their lamps, and went forth to meet the bridegroom.
2 And five of them were wise, and five were foolish.
3 They that were foolish took their lamps, and took not oil with them.
4 But the wise took oil in their vessels with their lamps.
5 While the bridegroom tarried, they all slumbered and slept.
6 And at midnight there was a cry made, Behold, the bridegroom cometh; go ye out to meet him.
7 Then all those virgins arose, and trimmed their lamps.
8 And the foolish said unto the wise, Give us of your oil; for our lamps are gone out.
9 But the wise answered, saying, Not so; lest there be not enough for us and you: but go ye rather to them that sell, and buy for yourselves.
10 And while they went to buy, the bridegroom came; and they that were ready went in with him to the marriage: and the door was shut.
11 Afterward came also the other virgins, saying, Lord, Lord, open to us.

12 But he answered and said, Verily I say unto you, I know you not.

While we may argue over the details, e.g., what the oil represents, etc., there is one aspect of the parable that is beyond dispute. All the virgins are Christians. They all believe and profess that Jesus is their Savior. We know this because they refer to Him as "Lord," they are looking forward to His return, and their lamps are lit. They have prepared for His return, some better than others. But they all believe in Him, and expect that upon his return He will gather the faithful for a wedding feast. To put it bluntly, believing that Jesus is the Christ will not suffice for one to gain entrance to the wedding supper of the Lamb.

Matthew 7:21-29

21 Not every one that saith unto me, Lord, Lord, shall enter into the kingdom of heaven; but he that doeth the will of my Father which is in heaven.
22 Many will say to me in that day, Lord, Lord, have we not prophesied in thy name? and in thy name have cast out devils? and in thy name done many wonderful works?
23 And then I will profess unto them, I never knew you: depart from me, ye that work iniquity.

What did they lack? They were Christians. They believed that Jesus was the Christ. They professed Jesus to be their Lord, apparently with considerable enthusiasm. They had done many wonderful works in His name, or thought they had. I can't believe they were lying about that to the Lord's face. And these works weren't just mowing an elderly neighbor's lawn; they were prophesying and casting out devils in Christ's name. They were expecting a "well done" and a warm embrace. But what they got was "depart from me, ye that work iniquity." Does that strike you as being a little harsh?

So, we've arrived at the crux of the matter. It being true that: "There is none other name under heaven given among men, whereby we must be saved;"[15] and "There cannot any unclean thing enter into the kingdom of God;"[16] and "Strait is the gate, and narrow is the way, which leadeth unto life, and few there be that find it;"[17] and "Not everyone that saith unto me, Lord, Lord, shall enter into the kingdom of heaven;"[18] and "Many are called, but few are chosen;"[19] then, what must we do--we who have felt the call to follow Jesus--in order to enter into the kingdom of heaven, in order to be chosen?

The debate is usually framed thus: saved by faith alone, or saved by faith and works. Is it not apparent, based on the two passages from Matthew quoted above, that neither holds true? The five foolish virgins had faith, and the "Lord, Lord" crowd had faith and works; and both groups came up short. Certainly, believing alone is not going to get it done. And I don't know anyone who believes that works alone will get it done; that's utter folly. But, unfortunately, believing and good works combined can still leave one on the outside looking in. Therefore, if it's not about faith, and it's not about works, and it's not about the two combined, what must we do?

As Jesus explained to Nicodemus in John 3:1-11, we must undergo the transformation that can only be accomplished by receiving the gift of the Holy Ghost and enduring to the end in the process of being reborn, of becoming a new creature. The transformative power of the constant and continuing presence of the Holy Ghost is the only possible way for us to become one with God (see John 17). We must think Christ's thoughts, do His deeds, develop His love for all mankind. Only the gift of the Holy Ghost enables us to do that. The Holy Ghost effects this fundamental change in character as we love and serve those around us, as we sacrifice to bring souls to Christ and build up His kingdom upon the earth, and do it while faithfully enduring the trials of life to the end--trials that a loving Father in heaven has custom-designed to facilitate this mighty change in us. It can't be done otherwise. And although this change may be remarkably apparent while we are in this life, it will not be completed while we are in this life. Nevertheless, we must have begun the process and have continued to endure in that process unto the end. **Then**, God's grace is sufficient, we are pronounced clean, and we are found worthy by virtue of Christ's merits, because God knows that we will continue to progress in the pure love of Christ, embracing all that is just and true--that the light within us will grow "brighter and brighter until the perfect day." An ancient American prophet summed it up this way in the Book of Mormon: "We know that it is by grace that we are saved, **after all we can do**." (2 Nephi 25:23)

How Does One Receive
the Gift of the Holy Ghost?

After being baptized by the authority of the holy priesthood, the gift of the Holy Ghost is received by the laying on of hands--and not just any hands--the hands of God's chosen and authorized servants who hold the keys of the kingdom. This authority, this priesthood, this set of keys of the kingdom, and this gift of the Holy Ghost can only be found in The Church of Jesus Christ of Latter-day Saints. This is the same authority, the same priesthood, the same set of keys of the kingdom, and the same gift of the Holy Ghost that was found in The Church of Jesus Christ of Former-day Saints. The scriptures below unquestionably demonstrate that in Christ's original church the pattern of the laying on of hands for the bestowal of the gift of the Holy Ghost was the established practice.

Acts 8:14-21

14 Now when the apostles which were at Jerusalem heard that Samaria had received the word of God, they sent unto them Peter and John:
15 Who, when they were come down, prayed for them, that they might receive the Holy Ghost:
16 (For as yet he was fallen upon none of them: only they were baptized in the name of the Lord Jesus.)
17 Then laid they their hands on them, and they received the Holy Ghost.

18 And when Simon saw that through laying on of the apostles' hands the Holy Ghost was given, he offered them money,

19 Saying, Give me also this power that on whomsoever I lay hands, he may receive the Holy Ghost.

20 But Peter said unto him, Thy money perish with thee, because thou hast thought that the gift of God may be purchased with money.

21 Thou hast neither part nor lot in this matter: for thy heart is not right in the sight of God.

Is it not apparent from this passage of scripture that being baptized, even by God's authorized servants, was not sufficient of itself for the new converts to receive the gift of the Holy Ghost spontaneously? Nor did they receive the gift of the Holy Ghost immediately after the apostles had prayed for them to receive it. They only received it when God's authorized servants laid their hands upon their heads, after they had been baptized by that same authority. There are two recorded exceptions to this pattern in the New Testament, and both are the result of new doctrine being introduced, before a pattern and standard practice had been established.

The first is found in John 20:22, when Jesus appeared for the first time to His gathered disciples after His resurrection; rather than lay His hands on their heads (ostensibly because they were not to receive the gift of the Holy Ghost at that moment), "he breathed on them and saith unto them, Receive ye the Holy Ghost." Then, His disciples had to wait 50 days

(40 days into which Jesus ascended to the Father) before they actually received the gift of the Holy Ghost on the day of Pentecost.

[N.B. John the Baptist was told by God how he would recognize the Christ, as recorded in John 1:32-33, "And John bare record, saying, I saw the Spirit descending from heaven like a dove, and it abode upon him. And I knew him not: but he that sent me to baptize with water, the same said unto me, Upon whom thou shalt see the Spirit descending, **and remaining on him**, the same is he which baptizeth with the Holy Ghost." It was vital that only Jesus had the constant presence of the Holy Ghost during his ministry, so that all the people might be drawn to Him, and to no other. John the Baptist understood this, and knew that he had to be removed from the equation once the Christ had come, saying in John 3:30, "He must increase, but I must decrease." In the meridian of time, only after Christ's ministry on the Earth was completed, was the constant presence of the Holy Ghost granted to anyone else. First the apostles received it on the day of Pentecost, and then by the laying on of their hands, all those who were baptized into Christ's church received the gift of the Holy Ghost so that they could follow in the Lord's footsteps, becoming a light unto the world by being valiant in the testimony of Jesus, both in word and deed.]

The other exception is the case of Cornelius found in the 10th chapter of Acts. In this instance, the Holy Ghost interacted with the gentiles for the first time in order to convince Peter that they were acceptable before God. This was necessary because, before that event, the apostles would not so much as break bread with the gentiles (in keeping with Christ's instruction and example, see Matthew 10:5-6 & 15:24), much less baptize them and lay their hands on them to bestow the gift of the Holy Ghost. Although the passage in Acts reads that the gentiles received "**the** gift of the Holy Ghost," this is a reference to their temporarily receiving "**a** gift of the Holy Ghost" (one of many), namely the gift of tongues. It is a case of their having an experience with the Holy Ghost before baptism (as they at that time had not been--but subsequently were-- baptized). This point is further elucidated in Acts 11:15, when Peter, as he is recounting to the brethren at Jerusalem what had occurred with Cornelius and the gentiles, says, "And as I began to speak, the Holy Ghost fell on them, **as on us at the beginning.**" This is clearly a reference to an experience the disciples had with the Holy Ghost in the beginning when they first began to believe in and follow Jesus. And, it is clearly not a reference to the day of Pentecost which took place long after "the beginning."

Both modern revelation and the New Testament indicate that while one may have temporary experiences with the Holy Ghost before baptism, the continuing presence of the Holy Ghost, or gift of the Holy Ghost, may only be bestowed after baptism. The Spirit of God will not dwell in anyone who has not been cleansed from sin by baptism. In Doctrine and Covenants 130:23, we read, "A man may receive the Holy Ghost, and it may descend upon him and not tarry with him." As for the New Testament, the process in its proper order was outlined on the day of Pentecost in Acts 2:38, "Then Peter said unto them, Repent, and be baptized every one of you in the name of Jesus Christ for the remission of sins, and ye shall receive the gift of the Holy Ghost."

Additionally, the following scripture found later in Acts, well after the events surrounding Cornelius and the conversion of the first gentiles, shows that there was no change to the pattern that had been witnessed in Samaria (before the gentiles were converted). In other words, after the first gentiles had their experience with the Holy Ghost, the disciples of Christ did not then alter the practice of the laying on of hands for the bestowal of the gift of the Holy Ghost after baptism. The pattern **did not** then become that the gift of the Holy Ghost bestowed itself spontaneously upon believers before they were baptized. Paul's recorded actions confirm that the laying on of hands for the bestowal of the gift of the Holy Ghost--and importantly, only after baptism-- continued to be the established practice of Christ's original Church.

Acts 19:1-6

1 Paul . . . came to Ephesus: and finding certain disciples,
2 He said unto them, Have ye received the Holy Ghost since ye believed? And they said unto him, We have not so much as heard whether there be any Holy Ghost.

3 And he said unto them, Unto what then were ye baptized? And they said, Unto John's baptism.

4 Then said Paul, John verily baptized with the baptism of repentance, saying unto the people, that they should believe on him which should come after him, that is, on Christ Jesus.

5 When they heard this, they were baptized in the name of the Lord Jesus.

6 And when Paul had laid his hands upon them, the Holy Ghost came on them; and they spake with tongues, and prophesied.

And also, in 2 Timothy 1:6, to his "son in the faith," Paul writes, "Wherefore I put thee in remembrance that thou stir up the gift of God, which is in thee by the putting on of my hands."

An Experience with the Holy Ghost Versus the Gift of the Holy Ghost

While the authors of the New Testament did not, in any one given verse (none that has survived anyway), clearly enunciate the distinction between having an experience with the Holy Ghost and receiving the gift of the Holy Ghost, that distinction is evident in the text of the New Testament when taken as a whole. Consider the New Testament reports of those who had experiences with the Holy Ghost before the day of Pentecost. We read in Luke 2:25-26, "And, behold, there was a man in Jerusalem, whose name was Simeon; and the same man was just and devout, waiting for the consolation of Israel: and the Holy Ghost was upon him [but he did not have the gift of the Holy Ghost]. And it was revealed unto him by the Holy Ghost, that he should not see death, before he had seen the Lord's Christ." Also in Luke 1:35 we read (in reference to Mary), "And the angel answered and said unto her, the Holy Ghost shall come upon thee, and the power of the Highest shall overshadow thee: therefore also that holy thing which shall be born of thee shall be called the Son of God." And again in Luke 1:41, "And it came to pass, that, when Elisabeth heard the salutation of Mary, the babe [unborn John the Baptist] leaped in her womb: and Elisabeth was filled with the Holy Ghost." (This is in keeping with the promise made by the angel Gabriel to Elisabeth's husband, Zacharias, in Luke 1:15, that his son, John, would "be filled with the Holy Ghost from his mother's womb.") Also in Luke 1:67 we read, "And his father Zacharias was filled with the Holy Ghost, and prophesied."

And yet, in John 7:38-39, we read John's parenthetical commentary concerning the words of Jesus, which clearly states that the Holy Ghost had not yet been given [perforce a reference to the gift of the Holy Ghost], "He that believeth on me, as the scripture hath said, out of his belly shall flow rivers of living water. (But this spake he of the Spirit, which they that believe on him should receive: for the Holy Ghost was not yet given; because that Jesus was not yet glorified.)" And again, clearly speaking of the gift of the Holy Ghost, in John 14:26 Jesus says, "But the Comforter, which is the Holy Ghost whom the Father will send in my name, he shall teach you all things, and bring all things to your remembrance, whatsoever I have said unto you."

Additionally, we should also revisit the three previously mentioned instances found in the New Testament (although, undoubtedly there were many others) where the disciples of Christ had experiences with the Holy Ghost during the Lord's earthly ministry, before the day of Pentecost. The first was the experience that Peter had--during which the Father revealed to him by the Holy Ghost who Jesus was--which enabled him to make his bold declaration, "Thou art the Christ, the son of the living God." The second instance being that of the two disciples on the road to Emmaus as recorded in Luke 24:32. In reference to the resurrected Lord, we read, "And they said one to another, Did not our heart burn within us by the way, and while he opened to us the scriptures?" This clearly implies that His disciples had felt the Holy Ghost cause their hearts to burn within them when they were in Jesus' presence listening to Him expound the Scriptures at some earlier time. That's why they reacted the way they did upon finally recognizing the Lord based on His manner as He broke and blessed bread while they shared a meal together upon arriving at their destination. They reasoned among themselves that they should have recognized Him earlier, based on the familiar burning in their bosoms that they had felt along the way. And the third instance is that mentioned above in Acts 11:15, when Peter, referring to the gentiles having their first experience with the Holy Ghost, said, "And as I began to speak, the Holy Ghost fell on them, as on us at the beginning. (Again, clearly a reference to an experience they had in the beginning when they first began to believe in and follow Jesus, and not a reference to the day of Pentecost.)

While there is some wishful thinking among those who lack the authority of the holy priesthood, who--of necessity--preach that said authority is not required for one to bestow the gift of the Holy Ghost, the Lord puts the matter to rest as He lists the responsibilities of those who hold the holy priesthood in Doctrine and Covenants 20:41. They are "to confirm those who are baptized into the church, by the laying on of hands for the baptism of fire and the Holy Ghost, according to the scriptures."

Others may argue the point; but as one who has had experiences with the Holy Ghost, and then subsequently received the gift of the Holy Ghost by the laying on of hands by God's authorized servants, I testify to you again, that there is a striking and vital difference. Before baptism and the laying on of hands by God's authorized servants, the Holy Ghost may enter into one's soul, but will not remain to dwell there. This leaves one with the calming assurance that God exists and that Jesus is His only begotten Son and our Savior, but without the continuing transformative power of the gift of the Holy Ghost. After baptism and the laying on of hands by God's authorized servants, the Holy Ghost enters into one's soul, and there remains, or dwells--so long as one is striving to keep the commandments of God--to undertake the process of making that person into a new creature. This transformation may only begin in earnest after one has received the gift of the Holy Ghost. We must have the Holy Ghost's constant influence to enlighten us, to bring to our remembrance the words of Jesus and his authorized servants, to comfort us, to burn out the worldly dross that encumbers our souls daily, until our thoughts become His thoughts, and our actions align with God's will.

The State of Christendom Without the Restoration

Out of all the members of the various denominations of Christianity (excepting the LDS church), those who faithfully strive to follow Christ today are comparable to the early disciples of Jesus. They had had experiences with the Holy Ghost, by which they knew that Jesus was the Christ; but they had not, while Christ was still with them, received the gift of the Holy Ghost. Shortly before His crucifixion, Jesus said to His disciples in John 16:7 & 12-14, "Nevertheless, I tell you the truth; It is expedient for you that I go away: for if I go not away, the Comforter [gift of the Holy Ghost] will not come unto you: but if I depart I will send him unto you . . . **I have many things to say unto you, but ye cannot bear them now.** Howbeit when he, the Spirit of truth [gift of the Holy Ghost] is come, he will guide you into all truth: for he shall not speak of himself; but whatsoever he shall hear, that shall he speak and he will shew you things to come. He shall glorify me: for he shall receive of mine, and shall shew it unto you. All things that the Father hath are mine: therefore, said I, that he shall take of mine, and shall shew it unto you."

After having been baptized, after following Jesus for three years, after seeing all the miracles performed and performing miracles themselves, after hearing all the sermons preached, after knowing by the power of the Holy Ghost that He, Jesus, was the Christ, and subsequently

169

seeing Jesus transfigured before them on the mount, in the presence of Moses and Elias, as the voice of the Father invited them (albeit only three of them: Peter, James and John) to hear His beloved Son in whom He was well pleased, after all of that, why could they not bear what Jesus had to say to them? Because they had not yet received the gift of the Holy Ghost. It is apparent, based on the words of Jesus above, that even after the additional 40 days of instruction that His disciples were to receive from Him after His resurrection--again, before the day of Pentecost--there were greater truths that they could not bear until they had received the gift of the Holy Ghost.

Jesus taught the masses in parables, and then, when He was alone with His disciples, He taught them His doctrine more plainly. Matthew 13:10-11, "And the disciples came, and said unto him, Why speakest thou unto them in parables? He answered and said unto them, Because it is given unto you to know the mysteries of the kingdom of heaven [a lengthy process that they had only just begun], but to them it is not given." Most of the teachings of Christ that are recorded in the Bible were intended for the masses. And even those teachings that He shared only with His disciples in private--including His teachings during that 40-day period after his resurrection mentioned above-- represented the milk and not the meat of His doctrine, which meat they would not be able to bear until they had received the gift of the Holy Ghost. And beyond that, we know that there is even greater light and knowledge to be revealed to the faithful, as evinced by Paul who, when he was caught up to the third heaven, "heard unspeakable words, which it is not lawful for a man to utter."[20] Apparently, one may only learn the truths that Paul learned there by personal revelation.

Joseph Smith and Sidney Rigdon put it this way, at the conclusion of the revelation they received together concerning the three degrees of glory, which is found in Doctrine and Covenants 76:113-119.

113 This is the end of the vision which we saw, which we were commanded to write while we were yet in the Spirit.
114 But great and marvelous are the works of the Lord, and the mysteries of his kingdom which he showed unto us, which surpass all understanding in glory, and in might, and in dominion;
115 Which he commanded us we should **not** write while we were yet in the Spirit, and are not lawful for man to utter;
116 Neither is man capable to make them known, for they are only to be seen and understood by the power of the Holy Spirit, which God bestows on those who love him, and purify themselves before him;
117 To whom he grants this privilege of seeing and knowing for themselves;
118 That through the power and manifestation of the Spirit, while in the flesh, they may be able to bear his presence in the world of glory.
119 And to God and the Lamb be glory, and honor, and dominion forever and ever. Amen.

As we read in John 16:12-14 (quoted above), the Lord said that the Holy Ghost "shall not speak of himself; but whatsoever he shall hear, that shall he speak." And to whom is the Holy Ghost listening? Why, the Father and the Son, of course, who are one in heart, mind and purpose. And in this manner "he will guide you into all truth." What would have become of the disciples of Jesus if they had said, "Enough, we need no more revelation. We have had experiences with the Holy Ghost, we need not receive the gift of the Holy Ghost. We know Jesus personally, we know he is our Savior, we have heard his teachings, this will suffice." If they had said that, they never would have been able to bear the additional truths concerning the Kingdom of God that Jesus had to share with them. Those truths He was only willing to share with His disciples after they had received the gift of the Holy Ghost, for only by that gift--the greatest of all the gifts that come from God--could the truth concerning all that "God hath prepared for them that love Him" be revealed to them.

Consider 1 Corinthians 2:9-14: "But as it is written, Eye hath not seen, nor ear heard, neither have entered into the heart of man, the things which God hath prepared for them that love him. But God hath revealed them unto us by his Spirit: for the Spirit searcheth all things, yea, the deep things of God. For what man knoweth the things of a man, save the spirit of man which is in him? Even so the things of God knoweth no man, but [except he has] the Spirit of God. Now we have received, not the spirit of the world, but the spirit which is of God; that we might know the things that are freely given to us of God. Which things also we speak, not in the words which man's wisdom teacheth, but which the Holy Ghost teacheth; comparing spiritual things with spiritual. But the natural man receiveth not the things of the Spirit of God: for they are foolishness unto him: neither can he know them, because they are spiritually discerned."

The Truth Has the Unique Advantage of Being True

But you may say, "What's wrong with my church? I like my church fine." Of course you do; you wouldn't be there if you didn't. But do you love the members of your church enough to be the pioneer who shows them the way to greater light and knowledge concerning Jesus and His plan of happiness for all who will follow Him--even though most of them will despise you for it, and only a very few will ever make the attempt themselves? You can always take solace in the fact that eventually they will all know that you were right and acted out of love.

Consider Matthew 10:34-37: "Think not that I am come to send peace on earth: I came not to send peace, but a sword. For I am come to set a man at variance against his father, and the daughter against her mother, and the daughter-in-law against her mother-in-law. And a man's foes shall be they of his own household. He that loveth father or mother more than me is not worthy of me: and he that loveth son or daughter more than me is not worthy of me." Knowing this, should we not then adopt the attitude of the Savior as found in Mark 3:32-35, "And the multitude sat about him, and they said unto him, Behold, thy mother and thy brethren without seek for thee. And he answered them, saying, Who is my mother, or my brethren? And he looked round about on them which sat about him, and said, Behold my mother and my brethren! For whosoever shall do the will of God, the same is my brother, and my sister, and mother." Furthermore, in Doctrine and Covenants 18:15, the Lord says that if you should "bring save it be one soul unto me, how great shall be your joy with him in the kingdom of my Father!"

But you may say, "I already know by the Holy Spirit that Jesus is the Christ." Wonderful! Now all you have to do is find out by that same Spirit that Jesus has again called apostles to whom He has given the keys of the kingdom, and that they are on the earth today. You are halfway home; all you need to do now is make the attempt to ask God to confirm to you that his church has been restored to the earth.

But you may say, "Anybody that reads Joe Smith's golden bible is going straight to hell!" I wouldn't know where to begin.

But you may say, "The Mormons may welcome all to their meeting houses; but they won't even let me in their temples, not after they've been dedicated anyway, what's up with that?" In this, you are misinformed. I can get you in. Trust me. I know a guy. There are a few things that you will need to take care of first; but it's doable. Shoot me an email. We'll make it happen.

But you may say, "No alcohol, no tobacco, no coffee, and no caffeinated tea? Are you kidding me?" All that stuff's killing you anyway, get over it.

But you may say, "Joseph Smith lacked the prerequisite

character to be a prophet." As compared to whom? Let's take someone we can all agree was a prophet. Christians, Muslims and Jews alike all revere Moses as a prophet. And yet, when God called him to be His prophet, Moses was on the lam for manslaughter, and he was guilty!

But you may say, "All right, but that's the Old Testament. Surely, you're not suggesting that Joseph Smith's character holds up when compared to the apostles?" Well, let's take the apostle without whom Christianity might well be just another sect of Judaism, Paul. He persecuted, imprisoned and gave his consent to the murder of the faithful followers of Christ; and then he was called to be an apostle. So, thank goodness Joseph Smith hired himself out to seek for and dig up buried treasure in his youth (as his detractors so often point out); if he hadn't, we wouldn't have anything to hang our hat on.

Most of those who reject his prophetic calling know next to nothing about the character of Joseph Smith. I've read from his journals, and from the journals and reports of his followers, as well as the writings of others who knew him but didn't follow him. I've studied his public records, public speeches and published writings, and the same of some of those who surrounded him. I have perused his surviving personal correspondence, including letters to and from his wife, Emma (which are filled with his tender affection and heartfelt concern for his wife and children). He was an honest, rough-hewn, faithful, brilliant (despite having no formal education), charismatic, patriotic, larger-than-life, fearless man who had the spiritual gift of a seer. Do you really think you are in a position to write off the restoration of the gospel of Jesus Christ based on what little you know about Joseph Smith?

This was a man with a grade school education who started out his adult life as little more than a day laborer. And yet he managed, in his short life, to: organize a religion; publish several books of Scripture which are considered to be the word of God by many millions around the world; and commission the gathering of thousands of industrious and faithful people from Europe and the eastern states to the western frontier of the United States where he--utilizing their collective skills--oversaw the construction of two temples, and turned a swamp-ridden, undeveloped parcel of land along the banks of the Mississippi into one of the most populous and beautiful cities in Illinois, named Nauvoo, in which, as the commanding officer of the Nauvoo Legion, he marshalled a state-chartered militia of 5000 men, before launching his campaign for the presidency of the United States in 1844. So, don't even think about muttering under your breath, "He was a bum," especially not you who spend an inordinate amount of time lounging around with a bowl of Cheetos in your lap, thumbing through Facebook while waiting for a rerun marathon of some TV show to start.

Consider the impressions of a contemporary observer who was impervious to the "siren call" of Mormon theology. Josiah Quincy, Jr. was a graduate of Harvard University (where his father had served as president) and an avid journal writer. He also served as the mayor of Boston from 1845 to 1849. In a book (published some 40 years after the fact, and drawing from his journals), he described his visit with Joseph Smith in Nauvoo in 1844, about 40 days before the prophet was assassinated. It is a fascinating amalgamation of admiration for the man and ridicule for his religious teachings. Despite being hostile to the religious precepts the prophet espoused, he had to admit that there was more to the man than met the eye. Since he has been called here as a character witness, we will consider his impressions of the man.

Having spent the better part of a day in Nauvoo with Joseph Smith, he wrote: "It is by no means improbable that some future textbook, for the use of generations yet unborn, will contain a question something like this: What historical American of the nineteenth century has exerted the most powerful influence upon the destinies of his countrymen? And it is by no means impossible that the answer to that interrogatory may be thus written: Joseph Smith, the Mormon Prophet. And the reply, absurd as it doubtless seems to most men now living, may be an obvious commonplace to their descendants. History deals in surprises and paradoxes quite as startling as this. The man who established a religion in the age of free debate, who was and is today accepted by hundreds of thousands [~16 million as of 2018] as a direct emissary from the Most High, --such a rare human being is not to be disposed of by pelting his memory with unsavory epithets. Fanatic, imposter, charlatan, he may have been; but these hard names furnish no solution to the problem he presents to us. Fanatics and impostors are living and dying every day, and their memory is buried with them; but the wonderful influence which this founder of a religion exerted and still exerts throws him into relief before us, not as a rogue to be criminated, but as a phenomenon to be explained."[21]

Recall the unsavory epithets that the religious leaders of the Jews ladled upon Jesus and His apostles in the first century: possessed of devils, winebibbers, blasphemers, liars who falsely claim authority from God, etc. Are we detecting a pattern?

Quincy's report includes an encounter between Joseph and a Methodist minister who was also visiting Nauvoo. Joseph was holding forth on the necessity of baptism for salvation, when the minister interrupted him to ask how that could be, in light of the Lord's words to the penitent thief on the cross, "this day shalt thou be with me in paradise." The thief had no opportunity to be baptized before he died. The prophet's supporters in the crowd were no doubt concerned that he had been tripped up. Joseph responded, "How do you know he wasn't baptized before he became a thief?" A good deal of laughter erupted from the crowd, much to the minister's chagrin. And here is where we see the true character of Joseph Smith in action. Rather than reveling in having vanquished his antagonist in a public forum, he rebuked the crowd with a glance, and assuaged the minister's embarrassment by explaining that the real problem was a mistranslation; instead of "paradise," the Greek should have been rendered "place of departed spirits."[22]

But you may say, "I'm just too far gone, my sins are so heinous that I can't repent." Really? Have you ever conspired to murder your innocent younger brother, but then settled for selling him into slavery, while breaking your aged father's heart, lying to him for years, telling him that the boy had been torn apart by wild animals? I didn't think so. But they who did that very thing have their names carved over the twelve gates to the celestial city as described in the Book of Revelation.[23] Joseph Smith said, "The nearer we get to our heavenly Father, the more we are disposed to look with compassion on perishing souls; we feel that we want to take them upon our shoulders, and cast their sins behind our backs."[24]

But you may say, "My sins are too embarrassing to confess." Get over it. It's not worth losing eternity over. (If you don't repent, your sins are going be shouted from the rooftops anyway, so, think it through.)

But you may say, "My sins are too deeply engrained, I could never overcome them to stand before God unashamed." You are right. You, on your own, cannot make that change; but you, with the constant influence of the gift of the Holy Ghost, **can make that change.** Oh, ye of little faith, repent now, while you are still on the potter's wheel, because once you have been fired in the kiln, it's everlastingly too late. Believe me when I tell you that God can make of you a new creature. This is His work and He's very good at it. You only need to participate wholeheartedly in the process that He has designed to bring you home, i.e., be willing to give up all your sins, live the doctrine of Christ, receive the gift of the Holy Ghost, and then endure to the end, pressing forward with faith in Jesus and the cleansing power of His atonement.

But you may say, "I don't have enough time left on the earth for it to matter." Consider the parable of the laborers;

those who labored all day and those who labored only the last hour of the day received the same wages. (Matthew 20:1-16)

But you may say, "Mormons are peculiar." You say that like it's a bad thing. Look around. 1 Peter 2:9, "But ye are a chosen generation, a royal priesthood, an holy nation, a peculiar people; that ye should shew forth the praises of him who hath called you out of darkness into the marvelous light: Which in time past were not a people, but are now the people of God."

But you may say, "I asked my minister about the LDS Church, and I was told it was all poppycock." Could that be because it's almost impossible to get someone to see the truth when their livelihood depends on their not seeing it? If the LDS Church is true, wouldn't your minister be out of a job? Standing before the judgment bar of God and saying, "But my minister and the religious scholars on TV said it wasn't true," isn't going to be much of a defense. It will be about as efficacious as saying, "But the Sanhedrin, the Pharisees and the Sadducees said it wasn't true." And God will answer, "My Holy Spirit was there, waiting to enter into your heart and testify of the truth; but you didn't ask, so you didn't receive; you didn't seek, so you didn't find; you didn't knock, so I cannot open unto you." In short, you didn't make the attempt.

To Make the Attempt

A young Joseph Smith fervently desired to get some answers about religion; then he read James 1:5, "If any of you lack wisdom, let him ask of God, that giveth to all men liberally, and upbraideth not; and it shall be given him." Afterwards he wrote, "Unless I could get more wisdom than I then had, I would never know [which of the many churches to join]; for the teachers of religion of the different sects understood the same passage of scripture so differently as to destroy all confidence in settling the question by an appeal to the Bible . . . I at length came to the determination to 'ask of God,' concluding that if he gave wisdom to them that lacked wisdom, and would give liberally, and not upbraid, I might venture."[25] So, what's stopping you?

I knew a certain Christian woman for many years, from my childhood. She would talk about the close personal relationship she had with God. I suggested that she take advantage of that relationship and ask Him if the restored gospel were true. She said that she did not dare make the attempt. When asked why, she responded, "Because I'm afraid I might be deceived." I asked her how close and personal could her relationship with God be, if she couldn't ask Him a question and then discern whether the answer came from Him or from Satan. She had no reply. I was saddened, knowing that she had buried her talent in the ground, out of fear, as did the unprofitable servant in Matthew 25:14-30.

Reasons **not** to make the attempt: fear of being deceived; fear of being ostracized; fear of offending friends and family; fear of having to change; fear of not being good enough; fear of finding out it's true because you've invested so many years in tearing it down; fear of insulting the memory of your ancestors (while in reality they are fervently praying on the other side of the veil that you will embrace the restored gospel, so you can do their temple work); fear of appearing foolish (1 Corinthians 1:27, "But God hath chosen the foolish things of the world to confound the wise: and God hath chosen the weak things of the world to confound the things which are mighty."); fear of having to endure the trials that may be required to perfect you . . . fear. 1 John 4:18, "There is no fear in love; but perfect love casteth out fear: because fear hath torment. He that feareth is not made perfect in love."

Reasons to make the attempt: to find out for yourself that the fullness of Christ's gospel has been restored to the earth; to know that the Heavens have been opened and revelation again flows between man and God as in ancient times; to know that the authority to make covenants with God that will be binding after death is again on the earth; to receive God's commandments, instruction, counsel and admonition through living apostles who are prophets, seers, and revelators; to have the ability to serve in God's kingdom and bring many souls to Christ (Doctrine and Covenants 4:4, "For behold, the field is white already to harvest: and lo, he that thrusteth in his sickle with his might, the same layeth up in store, that he perisheth not, but bringeth salvation to his soul."); to gather with the saints of the latter days who bear one another's burdens; to claim the Mormon Tabernacle Choir as your own; to have the privilege of paying tithing and receiving the great blessing promised in Malachi 3:10 (knowing that your contribution goes to build the Kingdom of God on earth, and not to buy a mansion, an expensive car and a lavish lifestyle for someone who only claims to be serving God); to enter into the House of the Lord and perform saving ordinances for your dead ancestors who died without accepting--or without a knowledge of--the restored gospel; and most importantly, to receive the gift of the Holy Ghost and begin the process of sanctification.

Don't Phone It In

When you make the attempt, don't phone it in. Don't just mute the TV and flippantly ask. Prepare yourself; then make the attempt. You have to "study it out in your own mind" and ask sincerely in faith. Read the Book of Mormon, attend an LDS church service and meet the Latter-day Saints there, have the missionaries over and listen to what they have to say, eliminate negative influences, turn off the TV, go a few days without alcohol and tobacco as a show of good faith, begin a fast, forgive those who have offended you, pray to know if the Book of Mormon is true while you are reading it; but save the big question--whether you should be baptized into The Church of Jesus Christ of Latter-day Saints--for last, the main event.

And remember to whom you are praying. That being that hears and answers your prayers is your loving Father in heaven. He has all power and all knowledge. He sees your life laid out before Him from beginning to end; and He shapes time and events in a tireless effort to bring you home. If you make the attempt, if you ask that God that gave you life to confirm to you, by His Holy Spirit, that it is His will that you should be baptized a member of the Church of Jesus Christ of Latter-day Saints, **you will receive an answer**.

In Conclusion

I don't think, I don't hope, I don't believe, and I do not opine; I know that The Church of Jesus Christ of Latter-day Saints is everything it purports to be, the literal kingdom of God on the earth. Jesus Christ personally commissioned it, He organized it, and He is the head of it today. And I know it by the power of the Holy Ghost. So, believe me when I tell you that you could never convince me otherwise. There is no tortured interpretation of Scripture you could present, no sophist's argument you could employ, no railing accusation you could bring against God's chosen servants in the latter days, no threat you could make that would have the least effect on the absolute certainty of this knowledge that I possess. You would have a better chance convincing Saul of Tarsus that he didn't see a light and hear a voice on the road to Damascus. I know that Jesus Christ is alive. I know that He is our Savior, and that "there is none other name under heaven given among men, whereby we must be saved."[26] I know that He continues today to do the work of His Father. And the work of God the Father, even Elohim, which is also His glory, is "to bring to pass the immortality and eternal life"[27] of His children--exalting all those who are willing to take upon themselves the name of His only begotten Son in the waters of baptism, and then "keep His commandments which He has given them; that they may always have His Spirit to be with them. Amen."[28]

Afterword

I have created a Facebook page, "Making the Attempt to Ask God," [https://m.facebook.com/Making-the-Attempt-to-Ask-God-1998289023784376/] for anyone interested in following up. It is a place where people who have made the attempt, and those who are contemplating making the attempt, can share their experiences, thoughts and feelings. Please visit the page and leave your impressions of the book, ask a question, or just peruse what others have posted. Via this social media platform, I will undertake to answer all sincere questions concerning the restored gospel, to the best of my understanding. There you will also find a collection of mostly color photos of people and places mentioned in the book.

Notes

1 *O Brother, Where Art Thou?* Directed by Ethan Coen, Joel Coen. Cannes: Universal Pictures, 2000.

2 Isaiah 3:16-24 KJV.

3 Clare Middlemiss, David 0. McKay, *Man May Know for Himself* (Salt Lake City: Deseret Book, 1967), 108.

4 Bruce R. McConkie, *A New Witness for the Articles of Faith* (Salt Lake City: Deseret Book, 1985), 262.

5 Joseph Alleine, *An Alarm to Unconverted Sinners* (England: 1671) 1st chapter.

6 Peter L. Crawley, ed., *The Essential Parley P. Pratt* (Salt Lake City: Signature Books, 1990), 164.

7 Matt 25:40 KJV.

8 George A. Smith, *History of George Albert Smith by Himself* (George Albert Smith, Papers, 1834–75, Church Archives), 49.

9 *Teachings of the Prophet Joseph Smith,* (Salt Lake City: The Church of Jesus Christ of Latter-day Saints, 2007), 255.

10 Ibid., 324.

11 David A. Barrett et al., *World Christian Encyclopedia* (New York: Oxford University Press, Second Edition, 2001), 16.

12 *Encyclopedia of Mormonism*, s.v. "Restoration of Melchizedek Priesthood."

13 Ibid.

14 The Complete Writings of Roger Williams (7 vols.; New York: Russell & Russell, Inc., 1963), V, 172, 220; IV, 371-72, 442; VII, 162-63, 167-68, 172, 176.

[15] Acts 4:12 KJV.

[16] 1 Nephi 15:34 BOM.

[17] Matt. 7:14 KJV.

[18] Matt. 7:21 KJV.

[19] Matt. 22:14 KJV.

[20] 2 Cor. 12:2-4 KJV.

[21] *Figures of the Past From the Leaves of Old Journals* (Boston, 1883), 376-377).

[22] Ibid., 391-392.

[23] Rev. 21:12-13 KJV.

[24] *Teachings of the Prophet Joseph Smith,* (Salt Lake City: The Church of Jesus Christ of Latter-day Saints, 2007), 428–29.

[25] Joseph Smith History 1:12-13 PGP.

[26] Acts 4:12 KJV.

[27] Moses 1:39 PGP.

[28] Doctrine and Covenants 20:77.

* 9 7 8 0 5 7 8 2 0 3 9 3 5 *